D0707424

The Essentials of
OBSTACLE RACE TRAINING

David Magida
Melissa Rodriguez

HUMAN KINETICS

CALGARY PUBLIC LIBRARY

MAY   2018

Library of Congress Cataloging-in-Publication Data

Magida, David, 1986- author. | Rodriguez, Melissa, 1980- author.

The Essentials of obstacle race training / David Magida, Melissa Rodriguez.

Champaign, IL : Human Kinetics, [2016]

LCCN 2016018707 (print) | LCCN 2016026270 (ebook) | ISBN 9781492513773 (print) | ISBN 9781492541486 (ebook)

  LCSH: Obstacle racing--Training.

LCC GV1067 .M34 2016 (print) | LCC GV1067 (ebook) | DDC 796.42/6--dc23

LC record available at https://lccn.loc.gov/2016018707

ISBN: 978-1-4925-1377-3 (print)

Copyright © 2017 by David Magida and Melissa Rodriguez

All rights reserved. Except for use in a review, the reproduction or utilization of this work in any form or by any electronic, mechanical, or other means, now known or hereafter invented, including xerography, photocopying, and recording, and in any information storage and retrieval system, is forbidden without the written permission of the publisher.

This publication is written and published to provide accurate and authoritative information relevant to the subject matter presented. It is published and sold with the understanding that the author and publisher are not engaged in rendering legal, medical, or other professional services by reason of their authorship or publication of this work. If medical or other expert assistance is required, the services of a competent professional person should be sought.

The web addresses cited in this text were current as of June 2016, unless otherwise noted.

Acquisitions Editor: Michelle Maloney; **Developmental Editor:** Anne Hall; **Managing Editor:** Nicole O'Dell; **Copyeditor:** Jan Feeney; **Permissions Manager:** Dalene Reeder; **Senior Graphic Designer:** Keri Evans; **Cover Designer:** Keith Blomberg; **Photograph (cover):** iStock.com/Nikki Bidgood; **Photographs (interior):** Neil Bernstein; **Photo Asset Manager:** Laura Fitch; **Visual Production Assistant:** Joyce Brumfield; **Photo Production Manager:** Jason Allen; **Art Manager:** Kelly Hendren; **Illustrations:** © Human Kinetics; **Printer:** Versa Press

We thank Pacers 14th Street in Washington, DC, for assistance in providing the location for the photo shoot for this book.

Human Kinetics books are available at special discounts for bulk purchase. Special editions or book excerpts can also be created to specification. For details, contact the Special Sales Manager at Human Kinetics.

Printed in the United States of America   10   9   8   7   6   5   4   3   2   1

The paper in this book is certified under a sustainable forestry program.

Human Kinetics

Website: www.HumanKinetics.com

United States: Human Kinetics
P.O. Box 5076
Champaign, IL 61825-5076
800-747-4457
e-mail: info@hkusa.com

Canada: Human Kinetics
475 Devonshire Road Unit 100
Windsor, ON N8Y 2L5
800-465-7301 (in Canada only)
e-mail: info@hkcanada.com

Europe: Human Kinetics
107 Bradford Road
Stanningley
Leeds LS28 6AT, United Kingdom
+44 (0) 113 255 5665
e-mail: hk@hkeurope.com

Australia: Human Kinetics
57A Price Avenue
Lower Mitcham, South Australia 5062
08 8372 0999
e-mail: info@hkaustralia.com

New Zealand: Human Kinetics
P.O. Box 80
Mitcham Shopping Centre, South Australia 5062
0800 222 062
e-mail: info@hknewzealand.com

E6624

The Essentials of
OBSTACLE RACE TRAINING

Contents

Exercise and Obstacle Finder

Exercise/Obstacle Name	Page number	Equipment needed
Glutes stretch	131	
Groiner	115	
Grip clench	151	Spring-loaded grip strengthener
Hand clench	150	Tennis ball
Hand walk	118	
Hanging knee raise	100	Pull-up bar
Heavy tire flip	163	Heavy tire
High-to-low plank	98	Mat
Hill repeats	78	
Hoist obstacle	69	Heavy weight, rope, pulley
Icy dunk tank	72	Dunk tank, ice
Intervals	77	
Jump and leap	71	Low barriers, wall, fire, or other obstacle
Kettlebell swing	104, 143	Kettlebell
Kneeling hip flexor stretch	129	Mat or pillow
Landing mechanics	126	
Ledge jump	73	Ledge
Leg raise	97	Mat
Log carry	62	Log
Low crawl	65	Obstacle to crawl under
Lunge	83, 142	Option: add weight
Lunge with curl and press	103	Dumbbells
Monkey bars	67	Monkey bars
Mountain climber	99	Mat
Over-under obstacle	66	Beam, wall, net, or other obstacle
Overhead squat	117	
Pinch grip raise	158	Weighted plates, anywhere from 5 pounds (2.5 kg) all the way up to 45 (20 kg) per hand

(continued)

Exercise and Obstacle Finder *(continued)*

Exercise/Obstacle Name	Page number	Equipment needed
Pinch grip squeeze	159	
Pinch grip transfer	159	A weighted plate, anywhere from 5 pounds (2.5 kg) all the way up to 45 (20 kg)
Plank	122	Mat
Plyometric training	137	
Power clean	145	Barbell or dumbbells
Pull-up	93	Pull-up bar, chair
Push-up	88	
Reverse lunge with twist	116	Dumbbell or kettlebell
Rolling mud hill or pit	71	Mud hill or pit
Rope climb	67, 152	Rope
Rope traverse	68	Rope
Rowing	81	Rowing machine
Sandbag carry	61, 160	Traditional sandbag, sandbell, or similar equipment in which you can grip with thumb and fingers
Seal walk	125	5- or 10-pound (2.5-5 kg) plate, sliding disc, ab roller, or paper plate
Shoulder press	92	Dumbbells
Side-to-side leg swing	111	
Side lunge	114	
Single-leg balance with reach	120	
Single-leg squat	121	
Spear throw	72	Spear
Spiderman climber	119	
Squat	84, 141	Option: add weight
Squat on a balance mat	122	Balance mat, pillow, BOSU, or similar unsteady surface
Squat with shoulder press	102	Dumbbells or barbell

Preface

It was early January 2011, and I had just finished my first semester of graduate school. Those first few months had been a blur, spent mostly in the library buried in books and assignments. It marked the longest period I had ever gone without exercising.

Normally a fitness junkie, I felt I just didn't have the time, focus, or energy for it. I watched my physique slip to a very puffy version of myself. My strength and cardiorespiratory fitness were at all-time lows, and I didn't seem to have the motivation to change it. I began to sense that my body was undergoing the change that so many millions of Americans experience in their mid-20s as their metabolism slows and they begin their 20-plus-year indentured servitude to society, sitting behind a desk for 10 hours each day.

And then, out of nowhere, my life changed. I was in the library doing research like a good grad student when I came across an advertisement for something called Spartan Race.

My interest piqued, I clicked the link, only to see images of people splashing through waist-deep mud, crawling under barbed wire, climbing ropes, throwing spears, and, of course, getting assaulted in front of the finish line by the legendary and now extinct gladiators.

The next thing I knew, I was registered for the April race in Miami.

I had better start training, I thought to myself, and immediately began a rudimentary three-month regimen of running and doing push-ups and pull-ups. As I said, rudimentary.

When the day of the race arrived I felt confident. I had been running consistently for a few months, and as a former collegiate runner, I felt I could handle the 8-mile course without too many problems.

Unfortunately, I failed to take many things into consideration. It was mid-April in Miami. Instead of signing up for an early-morning heat, I opted to register for the 12:30 p.m. Students and Military heat to get the biggest discount. It was 97 degrees and quite humid.

Today, 2011 is considered the old days of obstacle racing, a time when minimal water was provided because people like Spartan Race founder, Joe De Sena, believed "marathons [were] just catered training runs."

Unaware of this, I toed the line with no water, no fuel, no electrolytes, and no clue what I was in for. One thing I was sure of, though, was the feeling in the pit of my stomach: that nervous sensation you get only moments before laying it all out there in the heat of competition. It was a feeling I hadn't experienced in years.

Suddenly, as the race began, the butterflies in my stomach vanished, replaced by a rush of adrenaline spurring me to movement. The next thing I knew, I was flying along the trails with the leaders, battling for control of the race as I had so many times before as a runner. Initially, the experience didn't seem out of the ordinary. Some running, some trails, some river crossings. And then I saw it in the distance: the 8-foot wall, growing larger and more imposing with each step I took. But the moment I leapt up and rolled over the top, I knew I had fallen in love with obstacle racing.

Of course, the race was by no means over. I still had 7 miles of rolling hills, obstacles, and mud to get through. And with each step I took, my improper footwear, lack of hydration, and insufficient training took a toll.

As I neared the finish area, my energy levels were fading fast. And that's when disaster struck. I approached an obstacle where the objective was to hit a target with a rock, but my stone flew high and I received a 30-burpee penalty. As I began the first 30 burpees of my life, something started happening to me that had never happened before: I hit the wall. My legs turned to mush and just stopped moving. Putting one foot in front of the other was no longer second nature. I felt agonizing cramps throughout my body. My system was depleted of water, energy, and fuel to burn. My eyes got heavy. Hearing and vision became blurred. My body just started to shut down.

So there I was, hitting the wall 200 yards from the finish line, trying to knock out a set of 30 burpees. After what seemed like an eternity, I completed the dreaded 30 and lumbered on toward the finish. I'm not even sure how I got there.

By the time I crossed the line, I was barely coherent. It took three bottles of water, a slice of watermelon, and a coconut water to bring my body back to a reasonable state.

I'll tell you, I hate coconut. Can't stand it. But I chugged that coconut water like it was the last drink I was ever going to have. I was that desperate and depleted.

Revived, I immediately looked back on the events of that day with an overwhelming sense of pride. "That was the hardest thing I've ever done," I declared. "When is the next one?"

That is the beauty of the sport. It kicks the crap out of you and you love it. It speaks to you because it challenges you. Tests you physically, mentally, and emotionally. And it doesn't matter if you're the fastest person out there or the slowest. We all go through our own personal hell on the course. And we get to share that bond of accomplishment when we finish.

Over the past few years, I've spoken to thousands of people, ranging from those who have completed a single obstacle race to those who have lost track of how many they've run. Regardless of their experience level, the response is generally the same: "I fell in love with this sport,"

"I'm addicted," or "I've got the bug."

I've been obsessed with obstacle racing since that first race. It changed my life. It gave me a goal to train for that motivates me to take care of my body the way it deserves to be taken care of. I've raced professionally for the past few years, competing in more than 70 events. I left my job in corporate America to open up my own fitness facility and become a coach. There I teach obstacle race training classes and regularly lead groups to compete in races. And, of course, it led to this book.

Obstacle racing has given me so much. It is my pleasure to give back, to share this sport with as many people as I can, to teach them to love it and to master it. That's what this book is all about: preparing you for the rigors of a race so you can enjoy it and get as much out of it as possible so that when you get out there, you don't make the same mistakes that I did.

If you will be racing for the first time, buckle up. You're in for a ride that is both exhausting and intimidating. But you will quickly realize after the fatigue subsides that you did something truly special. And you'll be chomping at the bit for another chance to race. I'm willing to bet that, just like me, you'll catch the bug.

—David Magida

In only a few years, millions have participated in obstacle course races (OCRs) and mud runs. Clearly, many have caught the bug of obstacle racing. Thousands have changed their lives. The sport attracts individuals of all fitness levels: former couch potatoes, gym rats, weekend warriors, and devoted athletes.

Along with the rapid growth of this sport comes a need to adopt sound training techniques and plans. OCRs are attracting participants who are new not only to the sport but to structured exercise as well. One popular organizer estimates that as many as 90 percent of OCR participants are sedentary, highlighting the importance of a safe, evidence-based exercise program. *The Essentials of Obstacle Race Training* is a comprehensive training manual for new and returning athletes preparing for their first race or training to meet personal goals for their next challenge. If you are a novice- or intermediate-level obstacle athlete, this book serves as your authoritative training reference and guide. Not only will you gain guidance from training professionals, but you will also learn from the struggles and triumphs of those who have participated in obstacle races.

Part I of this book begins with an overview of the sport. In chapter 1, you will learn about the fitness, health, and wellness benefits of participating in the sport. Chapter 2 examines energy systems, principles of load, proper assessments, and body composition needs applied to obstacle racing. Chapter 3 discusses gear recommendations for training and racing. Chapter 4 provides nutrition guidelines for training and racing.

Part II analyzes common obstacles and how to prepare for them. In chapter 5, you will gain a better understanding of the challenges posed by racing, obstacle-specific skills, and recommended exercises for training. Chapter 6 discusses endurance, perhaps the most critical component of obstacle racing fitness. Chapter 7 delves into the importance of mobility and balance. Chapters 8 and 9 cover power and grip strength, respectively. Each of the skill chapters in part II describes and illustrates training exercises, circuits, and drills necessary for overcoming challenges.

Part III organizes the exercises introduced in part II into training sessions and plans. In chapter 10 you will find several workouts to get you in race-ready shape, while chapter 11 organizes these sessions into training plans relevant to your goals. Training programs for an entry-level, intermediate-length, and advanced obstacle race are included, all tailored to help you finish your OCR of choice.

Part IV provides guidance beyond training sessions. Chapter 12 offers tips for choosing the right race for your fitness level, training timeline, and personal goals. You will also gain tips on injury prevention as well as mental training techniques in chapters 13 and 14. Chapter 15 guides you through final preparation the weeks, days, and hours before the race; it also contains tips on navigating the course.

Consider *The Essentials of Obstacle Race Training* your ultimate tool for obstacle race training and preparation. Although this book may serve as your personal fitness and training coach, you will need to invest the time and effort to complete training plans designed for your personal goals. May the following pages give you the confidence and foundation so that you not only finish but also conquer your first (or next) obstacle race.

—Melissa Rodriguez

PART I
BASICS
OF OBSTACLE RACING

1

Benefits of Obstacle Racing

Meet Chris. Chris just finished his first obstacle race. It took him more than two hours to reach the finish line of a 5K race. Even though he struggled with climbing walls, crawling under low barriers, and swinging through monkey bars, the thrill of crossing the finish line outweighs any embarrassment he feels. He knows he didn't prepare adequately for the race and underestimated the challenges he'd face, but Chris is considering signing up again.

Considering an Obstacle Race

You've seen the photos on Facebook: your friends crawling under barbed wire through a mess of mud, maybe a finish-line shot of that moment of elation and accomplishment, perhaps a picture of your muddy friends drinking beer. Everyone looks like they're having the time of their lives. There's a reason for that: Obstacle racing is fun—*really* fun. It's a life experience.

Obstacle racing, also known as obstacle course racing (OCR), can be truly liberating. Ditch the cubicle, get out of that suit, and feel like a kid for a day. It's an opportunity to harness your sense of adventure and animal instincts. It's a chance to test your mettle, to see what you're made of both physically and mentally. Humans have always striven to test their limits and capabilities. We still feel that yearning, and an obstacle race is so out of our element, so far outside of our comfort zone, that it fills that role perfectly.

It seems the masses agree. Nearly 4 million people took part in obstacle course races in 2014, an exponential increase from an estimated 200,000 in 2010, when the pioneers of the sport held the first few events.

Each year, obstacle races are becoming more and more accessible. Regardless of your skill and athletic level, you're likely to find a race nearby that is a good fit for you. Races range from three miles to marathon length, so there's an event out there that will bring you just far enough out of your comfort zone. There are countless reasons for trying a race, including improving physical conditioning and mental and emotional health as well as just having a fun and memorable life experience.

Risk Factors

The features that make obstacle racing exhilarating and unique also make it dangerous. Risks arise in both training for and participating in the events. It is important to train correctly to condition the body in an appropriate manner to withstand the rigors of racing and preparation.

During training, be sure to progress and increase your workload slowly. This can actually be one of the greatest challenges you face. It is easy to get caught up in your goals and try to do too much too soon. Overuse and overtraining injuries are quite common. (You'll read more about overtraining in chapter 2.)

The most common overuse injuries for an obstacle racer are shin splints, stress fractures, and joint injuries such as runner's knee and tendinitis. Any stress fractures that occur are most likely in the feet and shins. Improper form and technique, which are common in beginners, can also play a role in the development of overuse injuries.

Additionally, many people don't realize the impact that terrain can have on the body. Training on hard surfaces such as asphalt and concrete can add to the pounding your bones and joints endure and increase your odds of injury. Regularly encountering uneven terrain, such as trail running, can result in problems with the ankles and feet as well. Many of these issues can be rectified with proper footwear, which is discussed in chapter 3. Of course, we provide you with ways to prepare and train your body to avoid these overuse injuries.

During a race, participants face a whole series of additional risks. Dehydration, cramps, and heart events could occur at any time. Proper hydration and nutrition are absolutely necessary at all times during a race. And you should definitely consult a physician to determine if you are healthy enough to participate before signing up.

Injuries during the race itself are a distinct possibility. Ankle and knee injuries are the most common; bruising, cuts, and abrasions are also common. Often the knee and ankle injuries are the result of falling off an obstacle, such as a high wall or monkey bars, and landing awkwardly. They can also be the result of running on uneven terrain, where it can be easy to turn an ankle or tweak a knee by stepping on a rock or root or even in a hole.

Cuts and abrasions usually occur during low-crawl obstacles. You're likely to get scratches (sometimes deep) on your back from the barbs, which could cause scarring. But the knees often take a worse beating because the surface that racers crawl over often contains hidden rocks, which can bruise the knees and even tear the skin. These open wounds that are then exposed to dirty water can become infected, most notably with MRSA (methicillin-resistant staphylococcus aureus, an antibiotic-resistant bacterium that is potentially fatal).

There have been several incidents of head and neck injuries at well-known obstacle races. While there's no need to delve too deeply into the details, in recent years a participant broke his neck while diving headfirst into a shallow mud pit, resulting in paralysis. In another instance, a participant jumping from an elevated landing into murky water landed on the head of another racer, breaking his neck. The injured racer drowned and could not be resuscitated.

None of the preceding information is intended to scare you or deter you from racing. However, it's important to know the risks before jumping into anything new. With those risks in mind, you can begin the process of preparing for a successful first (or second) race (and ideally many more).

Throughout the following chapters you will be introduced to a variety of obstacles and physical rigors that you might encounter on the course. We provide sport-specific exercises and drills that will help you prepare, explain tricks to navigating the obstacles them, and assemble an entire training program that will help you achieve your potential. We teach you how to fuel and hydrate appropriately and what to wear to maximize your comfort and performance. Being unprepared is not an option!

We face injury issues head on by providing preventive measures and recovery techniques as well as teaching you a few mental preparation tips for before and during the event. And finally, we touch on a very commonly overlooked issue: race-day etiquette.

With these items in your back pocket, you should enter your first obstacle race confident that you will have fun and not just finish the race, but finish well!

Why You Should Race

We've touched briefly on a few reasons that you can benefit from running an obstacle race. The most obvious reason is that it can change your life. Training for and competing in obstacle races can enhance your overall well-being physically, mentally, and emotionally.

Physical Benefits

Competing in an obstacle race provides you with an opportunity to dramatically boost your physical health. You suddenly have a specific rigorous event to prepare for. Having a goal is critical in any fitness program. For some, that goal may be to complete the race. For others, it could be for the sake of competition, maybe even to win. But regardless of the exact goal, it generally leads to greater motivation, more sport-specific training, and a more consistent regimen.

Very few people show up to the starting line completely unprepared. They prepare ahead of time, adopting a mentality of "suffer now so I won't suffer on the day of the race." For that reason, from the day you sign up for a race, you can expect to see and feel physical improvements in your body.

Over the course of an OCR training program, the most noticeable change might be weight loss or weight management. As your training regimen progresses and as the race date approaches, you will grow closer to your peak physical fitness. Weight loss can be a simple result of increased training and possibly even better eating. But weight loss is only the beginning, and as you push toward your peak condition you will notice other physiological improvements, including enhanced cardiorespiratory conditioning. You'll find you will be able to run faster, farther, and with less fatigue. You'll also notice that your daily energy levels are higher. Your strength, power, and explosiveness will also increase; these are important aspects of conditioning to develop if you plan to have success in an obstacle race.

Balance, coordination, mobility, and flexibility will improve significantly as you prepare for race day, particularly if you previously had a fairly sedentary lifestyle. If you work in a seated position, such as in front of a computer, you will see tremendous benefit as your low back health improves, hips loosen, and hamstrings lengthen from the additional exercise and mobility work.

Finally, you will find that you will have increased functional fitness, which is fitness that is actually applicable to real-life physical demands. Activities of daily living will become easier. Lifting heavy boxes, standing on your feet for long periods, walking around, even playing with your children all become less of a strain on your body.

And obstacle racing takes this a step further by forcing you to apply newly acquired functional fitness. Generally a race will require crawling, climbing, running, jumping, changing direction, and maintaining balance. These movements are tools in humankind's natural arsenal, yet adults rarely use these skills anymore. And when you get out there on race day, if you prepare accordingly, you will place these skills into action.

Health and Wellness Benefits

When you sign up for a race, you're not just giving yourself the opportunity for physical improvement. There are countless mental and emotional benefits as well. Participation in obstacle races and the accompanying training can improve your overall health and well-being dramatically.

One of the most noticeable wellness benefits of an obstacle racing training program is a significantly improved immune system. Studies have shown that consistent exercise can flush bacteria and carcinogens from the lungs and accelerate the outputs of fluid wastes like sweat and urine. Exercise also accelerates the rate at which white blood cells and antibodies are pushed through the body, improving the body's defense against disease. These improvements may be physical, but it is also a boost for your personal life and your state of mind. Not worrying about being sick as frequently and missing work and social functions because of illness makes your life simpler and more enjoyable.

Stress reduction, as a whole, is another wellness benefit of establishing a training program. The exercise associated with training for an obstacle race can be a tremendous stress reliever. Regular exercise can help you clear your head, get rid of nervous energy, and allow you to destress. That destressed state often transfers to other aspects of your life, allowing you to be more relaxed, more focused, and less anxious. An obstacle racing training program can be integral in establishing exercise consistency both in terms of effort level and day-to-day consistency. So as your exercise consistency increases, your daily stress levels decrease.

Mental and Social Health Benefits

It's not just the training that can improve overall wellness. The race itself can prove to be fantastic for mental health as well.

Take a look at your life right now. It's possible that you have a fairly sedentary lifestyle. You have a real life with adult problems and responsibilities. Whether you like it or not, you are expected to act a certain way. And that means proper and professional.

Every day you head into your workplace and go about your routine. You may love your job. You may loathe it. But the reality is work has become a routine. It can grow stale.

You may yearn for some excitement, for something new. As mentioned earlier, that yearning may be to test yourself or unleash that inner animal. And maybe it's just to free yourself from the confines of an office, from work attire, and from behavioral expectations. You might just need to have fun and to feel like a kid for a day.

Obstacle racing can provide you with that outlet, that opportunity to climb into the mud, get dirty, push your body to its limits, maybe even bleed a little. And the best part? It's completely socially acceptable. Not only will nobody judge you for your participation, but it's encouraged! It may seem like everyone you know has completed one of these races by now. They come home beaming, showing off their medals and photos. Proud not just of their accomplishments but of having the courage to go out and try it in the first place. And they come back shocked at how much fun they had. Because that's what it's really all about: having fun, having a memorable life experience, whether it's purely for yourself or to share with friends.

Maybe that shared experience is as a team. A group from your office all complete a race together as a team-building activity. You help each other over walls; endure fatigue, filth, and a bit of pain; and then share in the postrace glory. It's a fantastic way to bring co-workers together.

Perhaps that social experience is supposed to be competitive. You go with your friends to a race and the goal is to test your mettle and see who is the toughest or the fastest. Or you go alone to test yourself against a field of unknown athletes because something is urging you to test your limits. Obstacle racing provides a healthy, appropriate outlet for you to release your competitive side. And for some, it's an opportunity to rediscover competitive spirit. Too many adults have forgotten what it feels like to compete with their peers in a purely physical activity. So obstacle racing is good not only for the body but also for the mind.

But the social benefits don't stop there. At an obstacle race, you can meet countless people who were looking for the same thing you were. Whether that's a challenge, a fun day, an opportunity to be a kid, or even an opportunity to slay some internal demons, you will find people at these races with the same goals and mind-set that you have. And it's possible you may develop a healthy social life as the result of attending these events. New friends will share the mentality that an active lifestyle is a good one, and you may find that this has a positive influence on your life.

Final Thoughts

Once you start obstacle racing, it won't be long before you catch the bug and experience first-hand why this sport has developed a strong core following. In this book, we'll help you prepare for your first (or next) race, reap the rewards of racing, and reduce the risks associated with this activity. Read on for more.

Training Your Body

2

After a harsh reality check, Chris now understands he underestimated the challenges of an obstacle race. Determined not to let that happen again, he resolves to prepare for his next race. To give himself enough time to prepare, he has scheduled his next OCR a little over three months away. Now he wants to take some time to learn the best way to train his body.

Now that you're sold on the benefits of obstacle racing, it's time to prepare for an event. You could scour the Internet for workouts and advice from OCR organizers, trainers, and other experts, but you don't need to do that because you have this book to guide you! Before you start training, it's important for you to understand the scientific rationale behind your regimen. This chapter explains energy systems, principles of load, body composition needs, and fitness assessments applied to obstacle race training. Once you've read this chapter, you will be able to explain to your friends why you are following this training plan and how your regimen will specifically prepare you for an obstacle race.

Energy Systems

Simply put, energy is the ability to do work, and this includes all human movement and activity. (And you will need a lot of it to get you through not only an obstacle course race but also the challenging training sessions leading up to your event.) Energy systems refer to the specific mechanisms in which energy is produced and used by your body. Like most mammals, you generate energy via three systems: phosphagen (ATP-PC), glycolytic, and oxidative (see figure 2.1). All three energy systems are engaged during all forms of physical activity. However, the extent to which each one is involved varies depending on the duration and intensity of the activity. To train effectively, an athlete engages specific energy systems relevant to the activity of choice; in your case, it's obstacle racing. Let's review all three energy systems as listed in figure 2.1.

Phosphagen System

First is the phosphagen (ATP-PC) system. If you remember biology class in high school, you recall that ATP, short for adenosine triphosphate, is a molecule that provides energy for all movement. Your body breaks

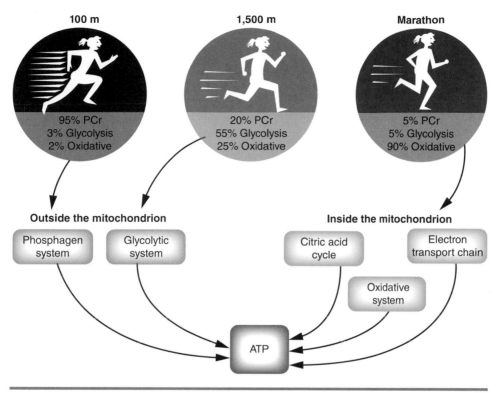

FIGURE 2.1 Energy systems.

down ATP to fuel your every move, from standing up to climbing a race wall. The phosphagen energy system harnesses ATP for highly intense activities that last 10 to 30 seconds. So for explosive activities like leaps over fire or jumps over a barrier in OCRs or sprints and plyometric exercises in your training sessions, your body is predominantly engaging the phosphagen system for energy. Since your body stores a limited amount of ATP, activities lasting more than 30 seconds must also tap into energy generated by the glycolytic system.

Glycolytic System

The glycolytic system uses carbohydrate to produce ATP. Activities lasting 30 seconds to 3 minutes are primarily fueled by energy produced by this system. Think of boxing rounds, which last 1 to 3 minutes. Soon, in your training, you will complete similar brief circuits, intervals, and drills to prepare you for some of the short, intermittent bouts of obstacles you'll face along a course, such as hauling a heavy object a hundred feet or negotiating a horizontal Tyrolean traverse over a stretch of shallow water. After a few minutes of sustained activity, your body starts to rely on the oxidative system to help meet your energy needs.

Oxidative System

Unlike the phosphagen and glycolytic system, the oxidative system is aerobic and uses oxygen to help with energy production. While the glycolytic system uses carbohydrate to generate energy, the oxidative system dips into other macronutrients as well: fat and protein. (You'll learn more about macronutrients in chapter 4.) The oxidative system is heavily engaged in low- to moderate-intensity activities. You'll harness a lot of energy via the oxidative system for your longer training sessions, including distance running. You'll also rely on the oxidative system to fuel you through the length of any obstacle race, from a 5K to a 12-miler.

WHICH SYSTEM MATTERS?

So as an obstacle athlete, which system do you target? All of them. An obstacle course race requires that you engage all three energy systems at varying levels throughout the race. To get through the distance of a race, you'll engage the oxidative system. To conquer a sharp, steep hill, you may need to tap into the glycolytic pathway, whereas a quick series of jumps call for rapid ATP production via the phosphagen system.

Unlike the demands of some sports, the challenges you'll face in an obstacle race are multifaceted. For example, a football lineman does not need to train in the oxidative system as much as an OCR athlete because of sport specificity. To prepare for the quick bursts of blocking and tackling demanded by the sport's position, a lineman may spend most of his training time engaging the phosphagen and glycolytic energy systems. However, this athlete may still engage the oxidative system for overall health and conditioning.

As an obstacle athlete, your training will give you the benefits of both worlds: increased sport performance and improved overall health. You will take on challenges through your exercise regimen that will engage all three energy systems. Speed, power, and explosive exercises and drills target the phosphagen system. Total-body circuits focus on the glycolytic system. Longer training sessions tap into the aerobic system. By targeting all three energy systems, you'll greatly improve your overall fitness and sport-specific conditioning.

Keep in mind that all energy systems are active at all times during activity. Your body stores a limited amount of ATP, so the three energy systems work together to provide the energy you need in order to keep moving. The extent to which each one is engaged varies depending on the duration and type of activity, whether it's an explosive move or sustained exertion over time. As you will soon see, the regimen outlined in this book will help your body improve its ability to train in all three energy systems so you'll be in race-ready shape.

Principles of Load

In sport and fitness training, load refers to any variable used to make an exercise challenging. For athletes, load is determined by the demand of the sport and individual goals. Load can be manipulated by more than just adjusting weight and the number of reps and sets. Modifications to the surface of training, such as standing on a single leg instead of both legs, and type of resistance, such as body weight or free weights, are also examples of load variables. To improve your strength and conditioning for any sport, your body must adapt to the stressors placed by load variables. Several principles are involved in devising a safe and effective training plan. For simplicity, we focus on five: specificity, progressive overload, overtraining, recovery, and detraining. See table 2.1 for a summary of these five principles.

Specificity

The specificity principle maintains that training should be relevant to the activity of choice. This applies to any sport or activity—be it obstacle racing or shoveling snow. Your training should develop the muscles

Table 2.1 Principles of Load

Principle	Definition
Specificity	Training should target the motion and muscle groups engaged in activity of choice.
Progressive overload	Load should be adjusted gradually so the body can respond and adapt to stressors.
Overtraining	Excessive or rapidly increased load on the body results in diminished returns.
Recovery	The body needs adequate time to rest and repair from training stressors in order to adapt to stressors and avoid overtraining.
Detraining	Prolonged layoff from training can lead to loss of strength, cardiorespiratory fitness, and other improvements made during regimen.

and skills you will need for engaging in an obstacle course race, which means you'll need to train similar patterns of movement and perform work in the energy systems you'll need to tap into on race day. Overall, the adaptations your body will make from the stressors of training will parallel the demands of the sport. Although this principle dictates that training should be specific to the sport, the actual regimen will vary across athletes based on fitness level and training experience. This is called individualization: A beginner working to get in shape for a first OCR will have a different regimen from a returning participant who is looking to improve on a specific goal, be it improving race time, developing upper-body strength, or increasing stamina.

Progressive Overload

While the principle of specificity emphasizes relevance of training, the principle of progressive overload stresses that the load placed on the body should be significant enough to illicit an adaptive response. In other words, if a few sets of push-ups are a breeze for you, you may want to try them with a weighted vest in an effort to strengthen your upper body and core. In order for your body to adapt and improve strength and fitness specific to OCRs, you'll need to train regularly. How often you train will vary depending on your fitness level and schedule, but for most of the regimens outlined in the book, you can expect to exercise at least four days a week. Since the demands of an obstacle race are multifaceted, your training will balance various types of training stressors—including running, core and strength training, flexibility, and mobility work—in order to give your body time to safely adapt. Finally, the principle of progressive overload also holds that loads should be adjusted gradually so as not to trigger the symptoms of overtraining.

Overtraining

Overtraining results when you've taken on too many stressors in your training, which includes increasing loads at a pace too rapidly for your body to adapt to or training too frequently, which does not allow enough time for your body to recover. Essentially, overtraining happens when you do too much. Your body will let you know when you've reached this point. Some of the warning signs to look for are diminished performance, lingering soreness after a training session, decreased willingness to train, reduced appetite, irritability, and injury.

Recovery

Recovery is critical in order to improve your performance and overall fitness. Your body needs enough time to rest, repair, and adapt to the demands of your training sessions. This applies to rest in between training sessions as well as after OCR events and even a sustained layoff after a competitive season. The amount of time needed for recovery varies based on fitness level, age, and exercise type and intensity. Beginners may need 48 to 72 hours of rest in between training sessions that focus on strength. Athletes at intermediate and advanced levels may use split routines for strength training so they can work opposing muscle groups on consecutive days (such as a strength circuit focused on chest and core one day followed by a strength circuit emphasizing leg and back strength on the next). For cardio-based activities, beginners may need only a day of rest, while elite athletes may engage in some form of cardiorespiratory activity most days of the week.

After a competitive season, athletes may take a long break—up to a month—to mentally and physically recover from season-long wear and tear. Although obstacle racing can be a year-round sport in some geographical regions, the off-season generally lasts three to four months because most obstacle events take place between March and October. So if you have several events planned then, it may be a good idea to scale back around the holiday months. One of the important things to keep in mind regarding recovery, especially a prolonged layoff, is that recovery doesn't mean you do nothing. It's not an excuse to lie on the couch with potato chips and beer. You can still exercise and focus on flexibility and mobility as well as maintain strength and cardiorespiratory fitness. Chapter 11 discusses the concept of active recovery.

Detraining

As you plan recovery in between training sessions and competitive events and as part of an off-season, keep in mind that an extended break from exercising may have a detraining effect. It's important to balance extended rest with maintenance work. Otherwise, you can risk losing some of the improvements you've made in strength, speed, endurance, and overall sport-specific fitness. And you don't want that!

Assessments

Obstacle racing is a unique sport that challenges several aspects of physical fitness. To complete an obstacle race, you'll need strength, core stability, and muscular and cardiorespiratory endurance. For this reason, you need a sport-specific set of assessments. The proper assessments will help you not only set a baseline for your fitness for OCRs but also identify specific strengths and weaknesses to build on and improve as well as track your progress. The assessments in this section will help you understand your current fitness level and pinpoint your strengths and weaknesses. Measure them every four to six weeks to gauge your progress. You can record your results in table 2.5.

Body Composition: Body Fat and BMI

Determining your ideal body composition will guide you as you get into race-ready shape. A healthy body composition is critical for sport performance, and obstacle racing is no exception. (See sidebar on page 20 for more on body composition.) Although, at the very minimum, you should aim for a healthy range, the ideal body composition varies across athletes. See tables 2.2 and 2.3. There may be some trial and error involved. Measure your body fat before starting your training program and before all other assessments.

You can measure your body composition in a few ways. Various tools such as skin calipers, body-fat scales, and handheld electronic analyzers can help you gauge body fat percentage at home. You can invest in one of these if you would like to track your body fat on an ongoing basis for your training and overall health.

Alternatively, you can calculate your body mass index (BMI), another measure of body composition, as a baseline. You can use this formula to calculate your BMI:

BMI = (weight in pounds / [height in inches × height in inches]) × 703

Then you can compare your results to the data in table 2.4 for a baseline. Be sure to record your results on table 2.5. You can update your BMI in table 2.5 on page 24 over time as you progress through your obstacle race training program.

Table 2.2 Body-Fat Percentages for Males and Females and Their Classification

Males	Females	Rating
>5–10	8–15	Athletic
11–14	16–23	Good
15–20	24–30	Acceptable
21–24	31–36	Overweight
>24	>36	Obese

Note that these are rough estimates. The term *athletic* in this context refers to sports in which low body fat is an advantage.

Reprinted, by permission, from A. Jeukendrup and M. Gleeson, 2010, *Sport nutrition*, 2nd ed. (Champaign, IL: Human Kinetics), 316.

Table 2.3   Body-Fat Percentage for the Athletic Population

Sport	Male	Female	Sport	Male	Female
Baseball	12–15%	12–18%	Rowing	6–14%	12–18%
Basketball	6–12%	20–27%	Shot put	16–20%	20–28%
Bodybuilding	5–8%	10–15%	Skiing (cross-country)	7–12%	16–22%
Cycling	5–15%	15–20%	Sprinting	8–10%	12–20%
Football (backs)	9–12%	No data	Soccer	10–18%	13–18%
Football (linemen)	15–19%	No data	Swimming	9–12%	14–24%
Gymnastics	5–12%	10–16%	Tennis	12–16%	16–24%
High and long jump	7–12%	10–18%	Track and field	5–12%	10–15%
Ice and field hockey	8–15%	12–18%	Volleyball	11–14%	16–25%
Marathon running	5–11%	10–15%	Weightlifting	9–16%	No data
Racquetball	8–13%	15–22%	Wrestling	5–16%	No data

Reprinted, by permission, from A. Jeukendrup and M. Gleeson, 2010, *Sport nutrition*, 2nd ed. (Champaign, IL: Human Kinetics), 316.

Table 2.4   Body Mass Index (BMI) Ranges

Category	Body mass index (BMI)
Underweight	<18.5
Normal	18.5-24.9
Overweight	25.0-29.9
Obesity	>30.0

National Institutes of Health National Heart, Lung, and Blood Institute: http://www.nhlbi.nih.gov/health/educational/lose_wt/BMI/bmicalc.htm

BODY COMPOSITION

Body composition needs vary among obstacle athletes, particularly recreational and competitive racers. If you are a beginner and your obstacle race is several months away, ensuring you have a healthy body composition should be your first priority. Keep in mind that as you train and fuel properly to reach a healthy body composition, you will also be working toward getting in the best shape possible for your obstacle race.

The body composition needs of a competitive athlete are defined by the demands of the sport. Obstacle racing requires endurance, strength, and power. For obstacle athletes running longer distances, a body fat percentage comparable to that of endurance runners and triathletes may be ideal. For those focused on shorter distances, a suitable body composition may resemble that of a sprinter or basketball player (who runs about three miles per game, or 5K, with a series of agility, power, and skill challenges mixed in). As a general rule, if you have multiple obstacle races planned over a stretch of several months, strive to maintain a healthy body fat range and fine-tune body fat in your off-season.

When you are in season, less than a month away from your race, it's not the time to focus on weight loss or body composition. Any rapid weight loss or drastic body composition changes weeks away from your event may actually deter your performance. Low-calorie diets while in training have been shown to negatively affect hormonal levels and place you at risk for stress fractures. In season, you'll need to eat enough to meet the energy and recovery demands of your training.

Strength: Pull-Up Max

Being able to do pull-ups is a prerequisite for crushing your obstacle race. Climbing over walls, ropes, and any other obstacle that calls on upper-body and grip strength requires mastery of the pull-up. Since this exercise is so important in obstacle race training, it's only fitting to make it one of your first assessments.

To do a pull-up, make sure you use an overhand grip and place your hands wider than shoulder-width apart over the bar (see figure 2.2a). Engage your abs and squeeze your shoulder blades together as you pull yourself up so your chin clears the bar (see figure 2.2b). If you can't do a pull-up yet, that's okay! Part of this training program includes progressions along with core, grip, and upper-body exercises you can do to get stronger. For the purpose of the assessment, if you can't do a single pull-up, just record how much of a pull-up you can do, be it one quarter, one third, a half, or any other fraction.

a   b

FIGURE 2.2 Proper pull-up form.

Muscular Endurance: Push-Up

As you've probably gathered so far, obstacle race fitness depends on mastery of your own body weight. Much like the pull-up and burpee, the push-up is a must in preparing for an obstacle course race. To test your muscular endurance, you will do as many push-ups as you can in a minute.

Be sure to do it right. Start with your hands and toes on the floor with your arms extended and feet hip-width apart (see figure 2.3a). Squeeze your abs and glutes to support your back. Lower your body as far as you can without resting on the floor (see figure 2.3b). Then come back to start. Do as many push-ups as you can in 60 seconds and record it in the fitness assessment log in table 2.5.

a b

FIGURE 2.3 Proper push-up form.

Core Stability: Plank

To crawl through tunnels, underneath netting, and below any other barrier, you need some core integrity to support your back and the movement itself. The plank is an ideal exercise for testing and improving core stability. To do it correctly, start with your forearms and toes on the floor (see figure 2.4). Squeeze your abs and glutes and tuck in your pelvis so your back is flat. Hold this as long as you can, up to 2 minutes. It may sound easy since you don't actually move, but don't be surprised if your whole body starts to shake after 20 seconds! Record your time.

FIGURE 2.4   Proper plank position.

Cardiorespiratory Endurance: 1.5-Mile Run/Walk

Conquering an obstacle race calls for cardiorespiratory endurance in order to last the duration of the race. To get a baseline for your cardiorespiratory endurance, run or run and walk 1.5 miles, preferably outdoors. Be sure to do this at the end of your assessments because completing a lengthy cardiorespiratory exercise may interfere with your strength and power output. Record your time.

Fitness Assessment

Use these benchmarks in table 2.6 to compare your baseline and progress. You will need to revisit your assessments in Chapter 12 when you learn how to choose the right OCR for you.

Table 2.5 Fitness Assessment Log

Fitness component	Assessment	Day 1	Day 45	Day 90
Body composition	BMI			
	Body fat			
Strength	Pull-up max			
Muscular endurance	Push-up			
Core stability	Plank hold			
Cardiorespiratory endurance	1.5-mile run/walk			

Table 2.6 Fitness Assessment Benchmarks

Fitness Component	Assessment Exercise	Beginner	Intermediate	Advanced
Strength	Pull-up max	<1	1-3	>3
Muscular endurance	Push-up	<10	10-19	20+
Core stability	Plank hold	<30s	30-89s	90s+
Cardiorespiratory endurance	1.5-mile run/walk	>18:00	12:00 – 18:00	<12:00

Final Thoughts

You've made it through the assessments. Congratulations! Training for an obstacle course race may sound complicated based on the scientific rationale behind training, but this book will guide you through the intricacies of OCR prep. This chapter gives you a better idea of the thought process and science behind your training regimen. Chapter 3 discusses gear recommendations for your training and essential items for your race.

3

Gear Recommendations

In addition to struggling with many of the obstacles in his first race, Chris found himself literally uncomfortable in his shoes and clothes on race day. He thought dressing for comfort—in old sneakers, T-shirt, and basketball shorts—would be appropriate. Instead, it felt like his "comfortable" apparel weighed him down during the race after sloshing through mud and traversing through water. Not again. What should he wear next time?

Using the appropriate equipment is an essential component of success in an obstacle race. From shoes, to shorts, to hydration gear, the proper tools can make or break your race. You'll have to deal with some of the harshest of elements in an OCR, so you'll want to be sure that you're equipped with comfortable clothes and shoes at a minimum. Convenient hydration items will come in handy for longer races. Let's take a look at a few essential items.

Footwear and Gloves

Properly equipping your feet and hands will positively shape your obstacle racing experience. Navigating through uneven and unpredictable terrain demands a lot from your feet, and you want to be sure to give them adequate protection and support to make it through the event. Since you'll need your hands to crawl, climb, and grip, you may want to consider glove options.

Shoes

The most basic item that any racer needs is good shoes. Fortunately, you won't make the same mistake Chris did. You have the benefit of knowing that you should be racing in a pair of shoes designed for an obstacle race or at least for trail running. Obstacle race–specific shoes didn't even exist a few years ago, but companies like Reebok, Under Armour, and Inov-8 have been quick to respond to demands by racers and have produced high-quality footwear.

When purchasing a pair of shoes for a race, you need to take several things into account:

- How long is the race?
- What kind of terrain will I be encountering? Will the course be muddy? Rocky? Hilly or mountainous? Is swimming involved?

➧ How wet will my feet get?

➧ What kind of obstacles will I encounter?

Each of these questions can influence footwear selection. The longer the race, the more support your shoes will probably need. Unless you have a lot of experience, you don't want to be in a race that lasts 5 hours in a pair of minimalist shoes or in shoes that you haven't taken the time to break in adequately. The soles of your feet might bruise. You might end up with some pretty nasty blisters on your heels, toes, and other hot spots.

However, if the race is only three to five miles, you can get away with using a shoe with very little support because you won't be giving them too much of a beating. Just watch out for rocks. Many minimalist shoes don't have much padding on top or around the toes, and you can really hurt yourself if you catch a rock. It's also easy to bruise the soles of your feet if you step directly on a sharp rock.

You may be saying to yourself, "There's no chance I'm going to be out there for 5 hours!" Well, I hate to break it to you, but if you run some of the longer races (10 to 15 miles) you might finish in 2 hours, but depending on the terrain it could take 5. So, select shoes with good support.

Your shoes will also need some serious traction. Typically, obstacle races are covered in mud, requiring shoes with large lugs to keep you stable through turns and hills. Those big lugs can get you out of jams, particularly mud pits and steep descents. Pick a shoe that has an aggressive tread, ideally one with rubber teeth on the sole like in figure 3.1.

FIGURE 3.1 Footwear with prominent lugs are critical for keeping your feet stable through muddy hills and sharp turns.

A good tread will minimize slipping, falling, and even wasted energy, allowing you to move faster and more efficiently over varied terrain.

The amount of water you'll encounter can have an impact on shoe selection. Although you want to wear a shoe with good support, a wet shoe is very heavy. Over time, it will wear you out, so choose your shoe accordingly. If you anticipate a great deal of swimming or even just water crossings such as mud pits, rivers, lakes, or areas where it rains a lot, try to wear a lighter shoe that's less likely to retain a lot of water. Inspired by the footwear a steeple chaser might wear, some shoes are even designed with holes to drain water. Others are made of water-resistant material so you don't waste energy and speed carrying unnecessary weight. The same could be said for mud, which can soak in and make your feet feel like blocks of cement. When choosing your ideal shoe, always consider the impact of carrying water and mud over the distance of your race. Odds are that you'll have to do so and you might as well minimize the weight you carry.

During shoe selection, it's also important to think about the shape of your foot. Do you have high arches? Flat feet? Wide feet? Some obstacle racing shoes have a narrow profile, in the style of cross-country racing spikes. Others are designed more similar to trail-running or off-trail-running shoes, with thicker soles and a wider tread.

Be sure to get your feet and gait assessed at a running store so you can determine the best-fitting shoes. If you have flat feet or exaggerated arches, consider consulting with a podiatrist to get recommendations on orthotic inserts. Also, if you have limited experience with minimalist running footwear, be sure to look for adequate cushioning in a racing shoe. The right racing shoes can be pricey, ranging from $90 to more than $140, but they will be a worthwhile investment.

Socks

If you're choosing high-quality racing shoes and orthotics, you might as well select the appropriate socks. Socks can be made of many types of material. Pay attention to length, too. You want to determine your selection based on temperature and the distance you are running as well as terrain.

If the weather is warm, you may opt for an ankle-length sock that is as light as possible. Make sure it's an actual dry-fit sock that allows your feet to breathe and doesn't carry much water weight. Having the sock reach at least the ankle is ideal because it can protect you from rope burn in a variety of situations, including rope climbs and traverses. Whether or not those socks have individual toes is entirely up to you, and if you ask the top athletes in the sport, they will give you a variety of answers about which variety is best.

Full-length socks can have their benefits, particularly if they are made of compression material. Opt away from full-length cotton socks because they will become extremely heavy and you will quickly become fatigued carrying them once they are wet. Using a compression sock can be ideal not just for its quick drying properties but also for improving blood flow in the legs. Some athletes believe enhanced blood flow can improve performance and minimize cramping. The long socks can also protect your legs during crawls and climbs as well as from stray branches while running. These long compression socks will only slow you down minimally, if at all, and will spare you from days of additional and unnecessary pain postrace. You have only one body, so take care of it. Less pain means more fun, and isn't that the point anyway?

If you are accustomed to it and the race isn't too long, you can even opt to race without socks. This option offers the least amount of protection for your feet and ankles but can be lighter and therefore allow you to run slightly quicker because you're not weighted down by water- or mud-soaked socks. Of course, if your feet take a turn for the worse with blisters, you will inevitably lose time, so it can be a gamble. In a longer race, if your feet take a turn for the worse, you will have a very long day ahead of you.

Heed our advice: If you plan on racing for many hours, proper footwear is essential. If you are shopping for an obstacle racing shoe for the first time, you may want to buy a couple different pairs and give each a test run through your training in order to see which one works best for you on race day.

Gloves

Although it seems like a nice addition on cold days, very rarely do I recommend gloves. There have been only a few occasions where I have raced in them, although they have occasionally come in handy.

Gloves can protect your hands from cuts and bruises, but with that protection comes compromised grip strength. Any time you put a barrier between your skin and an object, you are lowering your sensitivity and awareness. Decreased grip and a decreased sense of the object you are gripping can lead to obstacle failure.

However, sometimes personal safety or warmth is a deciding factor, and you must wear gloves. In those situations, I recommend using fingerless or tipless gloves (see figure 3.2). These allow your hands to breathe and provide you with added dexterity while still protecting your palms and the lower half of your fingers.

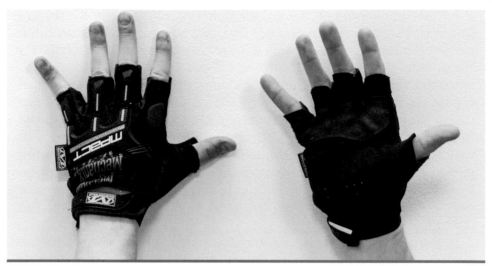

FIGURE 3.2 Gloves can protect your hands, but may interfere with your grip strength.

Men's Apparel

Just as in other aspects of life, men and women have different needs when it comes to racing apparel. For men, the most basic item of apparel is a good pair of shorts.

In obstacle racing, shorts are generally of two varieties. The first is traditional running shorts, often 5 to 7 inches (12-18 cm) in length. There are many benefits to racing in running shorts. They are comfortable, many people are used to running and training in them, and they are minimally restrictive. They allow room to breathe and are a time-tested option for runners.

However, you may choose to wear compression shorts for several reasons. The first is chafing. When running shorts get wet, they tend to rub fairly mercilessly on the inner thighs. The result is some pretty nasty chafing, which can bother you for days after your race. You will not face this problem when racing in compression shorts. These shorts protect your thighs by limiting rubbing and providing a layer of protection for your skin. They also keep grit and gravel from getting up into your shorts and scraping you.

The second reason to wear compression shorts is speed. When you exit the water, shorts can become heavy and burdensome. Compressions allow you to continue moving at the same speed without losing any energy fighting the weight of the water. It's one of the reasons triathletes wear compressions.

Another reason to wear compression shorts is for their wicking properties. During a race, you'll get muddy and wet and sweat a lot, and wearing clothing that lacks wicking fibers—like Chris did on race day—will only weigh you down. Compression wear can help you shed any excess moisture so you won't have to slow down on account of nonwicking apparel.

Finally, there's the concept of physical protection. For men, it's not just the legs that the shorts protect. It's also the man parts. As you navigate obstacles, whether it's a low crawl, a rope climb, or a wall, you can very easily sustain trauma to a very delicate region of the body. Compression shorts do a much better job than traditional shorts at protecting this area, providing cushioning and keeping everything locked down tight, so to speak. You can improve this even more by wearing a second layer under those shorts. Be careful if you don't wear a second layer because some compressions can become fairly sheer when stretched and you may become visible to the world. A second layer, such as a pair of athletic underwear, can also be useful if your compressions were to tear on barbed wire, a not-so-uncommon issue in this sport.

If the weather is very cold, you can opt for full-length compression tights. Those tights provide warmth as well as added protection for your knees during obstacle navigation, particularly crawls over rough terrain. However, this protection is only slightly greater than what you would have from compression shorts and long compression socks, and some people are bothered by compression over the knee joint, so opt for full-length pants only if you are comfortable in them.

Regarding shirts, many elite male racers tend to stay away from them. When they get wet and muddy, shirts become heavy and burdensome. They catch on barbed wire and can get in the way during some climbing obstacles, restricting the range of motion on shoulders and impeding free movement.

Most of the top pros opt to go shirtless, although a few will sometimes wear compression tops. Their reasons vary from trying to stay warm to using the shirt to avoid cuts and scrapes while rolling over the walls to simply wanting to show off their sponsors. However, choosing to wear or not to wear a shirt is a personal preference. You may prefer to stay covered. If you do, make sure to compare quick-drying fabrics as well as compression ones. Also, if you decide to wear a shirt to protect you from cold temperatures, an underrated but effective option is the nylon windbreaker. It dries fast, allows you to retain a great deal of body heat, can unzip to allow breathability if you begin to overheat, and does not carry much water. Plus, it can be removed and placed in a hydration pack (discussed later in the chapter) without taking up much room or weighing you down. This option can be particularly helpful for longer events when the temperatures have been cold.

Women's Apparel

Apparel needs for women are different from men's for obvious reasons. With the variety of athletic clothing available for women, pinpointing the right gear can be challenging. But thanks to the rapid rise of obstacle racing, several companies make apparel suitable for female obstacle racers.

Let's start with tops. A good sport bra is a must. As for most OCR apparel, it's best to look for material that wicks away moisture: usually synthetic blends of spandex, nylon, polyester, elastane, or proprietary fibers. Adequate support is just as important as material. Look for sport bras typically suitable for higher-impact activities like running, basketball, and plyometric training, because obstacle racing calls for running, agility, changing direction, jumping and landing, and similar high-impact movements.

For some women, a good sport bra is the only top layer needed. But for protection against barbed wire, stray branches, cold, wind, and other elements, an additional layer helps. If it's an especially cold or rainy race day, a windbreaker or race vest may come in handy. Again, we prioritize material that wicks away moisture. Compression or generic fitted tops, sleeveless and sleeved, are popular options, depending on weather conditions, preference, or extent of protection needed. Keep in mind the advantage of compression over generic fitted tops: Compression wear has been shown to help with performance by improving blood flow and keeping you dry. Generic fitted sport apparel will help keep you dry, but it doesn't carry the benefits of compression.

As for bottoms, your most important layer is underwear. There are lots of options in terms of styles, so go with what's comfortable for you. Underwear made of nylon, polyester, spandex, elastane, and similar proprietary blends with mesh should fit the bill. Fabric that stretches and allows you to breathe will help you move as comfortably as you can in a muddy race and will give you one fewer obstacle to worry about. Leading performance gear brands, including Under Armour, Inov-8, Athleta, and Title Nine, all make active underwear for women.

Next, shorts and tights. You can choose from running shorts, compression shorts, or fitted shorts. The benefits of compression and fitted shorts outweigh the benefits of running shorts, especially for wet and muddy races. Running shorts don't wick away moisture as well as compression and fitted shorts.

Should you wear shorts or tights? The answer to this question often depends on personal preference and weather conditions. Long-time runners taking on their first obstacle races may be more comfortable in running shorts. Beginners may want to start with tights for added protection for knees, shins, and legs. Some do both, combining tights with running shorts, but this isn't necessary and may actually hinder performance because you'll essentially have a second layer to contend with getting wet and weighing you down. Consider layering only for windy and cold races.

One final word on compression for women: If you're new to compression, be sure to look for apparel specific to athletic performance rather than undergarments intended for aesthetics or postsurgery (such as after a tummy tuck or C-section). While the benefits of both types of compression apparel are similar in that they both help increase blood flow, compression gear designed for athletes is made of materials specific for performance and recovery, supporting moisture-wicking and muscle mobility. This may seem like a no-brainer to some, but it deserves mention in ensuring you choose the right compression wear for OCR performance.

Gear for Hydration and Fuel Storage

Equipment for hydration and fuel storage is the final piece of the puzzle. There are three types for you to choose from: hydration pack, hydration belt, and fuel belt. The main idea behind racing with a hydration source is to ensure you have enough water consistently throughout the race. Concerns about distance, temperature, and lack of water stations may influence you to wear one, particularly if you are interested in storing fuel for the race as well.

Packs and belts, while useful, can also be heavy and burdensome and cause issues with obstacle navigation when you must move within the confines of a tight space. Low crawls, particularly with barbed wire, become tricky with a hydration pack and often must be navigated by first removing the pack and dragging it as you crawl to avoid damaging the bladder (the water receptacle part of the pack).

Depending on the length of your race, however, you may not need any of these items. For example, a 5K race with water stops might preclude you from needing to carry any of your own gear. If you are racing for less than 90 minutes, you likely don't need to refuel on your own but can wait until you complete the race to stock up on the goodies that await you at the finish line. We approach the topic of race fuel in depth in chapter 4.

Hydration Pack

The hydration pack is probably the most well-known item that obstacle racers use on the course. With brands like Camelbak becoming household names, they are certainly prevalent in races among open competitors. However, it is not often that you will see the top competitors wearing hydration packs, and when they do, it is only when the race is particularly long and brutal.

Hydration packs generally offer the ability to carry 40 to 100 ounces of fluid with you (1.2-2.9 L). The fluid could be water, a sport drink, or a combination of the two. The most common size is about 70 ounces (2 L), but size is completely up to personal preference. The liquid is contained in a bladder that sits inside a small backpack, generally fitted very snugly to avoid bouncing (see figure 3.3). Here are some things you want to think about when selecting a hydration pack:

- **Select a size that is appropriate for your needs in a race or training.** There is no need to carry a pack that is too large. The weight of it will gradually wear on you. But also make sure it carries enough fluid to get you through your race. There is nothing worse than running out of fluid when you need it most.

- **Pick a pack that is the right shape for you.** There are two types of hydration packs: actual packs that wear like backpacks and race vests. The packs can carry more and are a bit more practical but are bulky. Vests are a bit lighter and easier to run or move in but have a limited capacity both for liquid and for other items.

- **Find a pack that fits you as snugly as possible.** Running with a loose pack is not just uncomfortable; it's also inefficient. Obstacle racing is about efficiency. Every time your loose pack bounces up and down, that's energy that isn't devoted to moving forward. It sounds like a small thing, but we assure you, over time, this wasted energy adds up. Make sure you find a pack with a chest strap that buckles shut and cinches that tighten on the shoulders. Many packs are built with what is known as a propulsion harness designed to keep the bag stable even as your arms and shoulder swing as you run. Keeping the pack flush to your back will also spare you the discomfort of chafing on the skin on your back.

- **Select a pack that has some room for storage.** There are several reasons you need storage in your hydration pack. Electrolytes, fuel, and even a place to stick certain articles of clothing can come in handy. When selecting a pack, be sure to find one that has an easy-access compartment or two. Those compartments should be easily reached while you are wearing the pack so that you don't need to stop and remove the pack in order to access any items you might need.

Hydration Belt

Different from a hydration pack but similar in that it provides the ability to carry fluids during races is the hydration belt. Hydration belts come in a variety of shapes and sizes, but the most common options use one single water bottle or two flask bottles (see figure 3.4).

FIGURE 3.3 For longer races, some athletes carry a hydration pack.

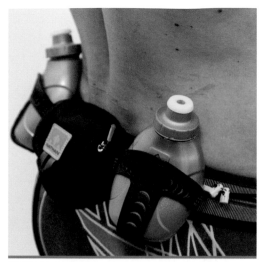

FIGURE 3.4 A belt with two water flasks is a common alternative to a hydration pack.

Hydration belts offer the benefit of being light and compact, holding the water weight to your lower back or hips so your stride is only minimally affected by the weight and shape. Navigating obstacles becomes easier with a hydration belt than with a pack, and many hydration belts still offer reasonable storage for food, gels, and electrolytes. The hydration pack is recommended for middle- to longer-distance races (8-12 miles or 12.8-19.3 km), where you may need water but only 12 to 20 ounces (0.3-0.6 L) to get you through the race.

The downside to running with hydration belts is that they are often too tight or loose in securing the bottle, making accessing and then storing your fluid difficult midstride or, even worse, allowing your bottle to slip out midrace. The last thing you want to be worried about during a race is whether your bottle will stay in its holster. But, if comfortable with a belt, you stand a much better chance of optimal performance than you do when running with a hydration pack.

Fuel Belt

Your final option is the fuel belt. Similar to the hydration belt in that it sits low on the hips, the fuel belt is the lightest storage option. However, the fuel belt does not carry any water. It is simply a small pouch enabling you to carry items such as energy gels, chews, and electrolytes (see figure 3.5).

The fuel belt is probably the best item for navigating an obstacle course and is recommended for races in distances varying from 3 to 10 miles (5-16 km).

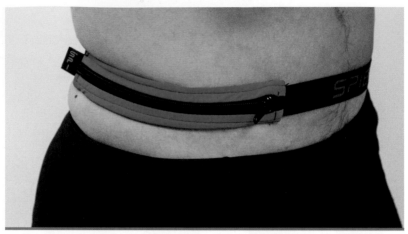

FIGURE 3.5   A fuel belt will help you carry chews, gels, and other compact energy items during a race.

We can personally vouch for the effectiveness of this item. If you feel confident that you can sustain your hydration simply off of the water stations, this item can be a valuable tool. It can also assist you in the completion of a few obstacles, including the rope traverse and bucket carry. We discuss these challenges in chapters 6 through 9.

Final Thoughts

Just as you are careful about your training, you should be equally careful about preparing your equipment. Take time to try on and select the best possible gear and equipment for your needs. These assets will make your race experience much more enjoyable. Regardless of what you choose to race in, always opt to train in the gear as much as possible. Never try out a new piece of clothing, shoes, or equipment for the first time in a race. You want to be comfortable running and moving in the equipment you've chosen. It makes a huge difference on race day.

Much of your training and racing gear will be based on your nutrition needs throughout the race. So please keep gear in mind as you review chapter 4, which covers nutrition applied to your personal training and racing needs.

4

Fueling
for Training
and Racing

Chris often asks himself this question: If I'm training regularly, do I have to watch what I eat? He's always believed that athletes have the luxury of eating whatever they want, but he recalls that a bowl of sugary cereal for breakfast might not have given him enough energy for his first race. If he has to, he wants to be sure he's taking in enough calories and nutrient-dense foods in order to get in shape for race day and improve his performance since the previous race.

Getting ready for an obstacle race goes beyond your physical training sessions. Although you'll exercise several hours a week, eating healthy takes up more time and possibly even more willpower! Some people think that because you're an athlete, you can eat whatever you want—all your hard work will burn off and offset any bad calories. That's not true. In fact, athletes may need to be more vigilant than nonathletes about what they put into their bodies. The good news is that eating well can be enjoyable—especially when it helps you meet your training and race goals.

This chapter provides nutrition and eating guidelines for obstacle race training and competition. It's no secret that sound nutrition improves your overall health and wellness. A healthy eating plan will also help you fuel properly for training and recover from rigorous workouts.

Nutrition Basics for Athletes

A healthy eating plan to fuel your athletic training starts with an understanding of principles of nutrition. In this section, we cover macronutrients (carbohydrate, fat, and protein) and micronutrients (minerals and vitamins). We also review the importance of water and briefly examine the impact of alcohol on an athlete's diet.

Macronutrients and Micronutrients

Most of what you consume can be broken down into macronutrients and micronutrients. Macronutrients provide energy measured in calories from carbohydrate, protein, and fat. Micronutrients do not contain calories (or have calories in very trace amounts); these are vitamins and minerals. Unlike macronutrients, micronutrients are typically consumed in very small amounts but support essential functions of the body. Let's start with macronutrients.

Carbohydrate

The main function of carbohydrate is to provide energy. Every gram of carbohydrate contains four kilocalories, also referred to as calories for short. When you need energy for an intense activity lasting more than 30 seconds, the glycolytic system supplies energy derived from carbohydrate. Your body stores carbohydrate in the form of glycogen in muscles and glucose in blood cells. So when you need to crank out a set of push-ups, your body is likely tapping into glycogen stores.

Although low-carb diets are practically a mainstay in weight-loss eating plans, they can be detrimental to athletes. A diet low in carbohydrate can affect not only your performance but your mood as well. Diets lacking in carbohydrate can lead to irritability, mental and emotional fatigue, inability to concentrate, sleeplessness, and even depression. For this reason, aim to get most of your total caloric intake (55-60%) from carbohydrate.

In addition to providing energy, some carbohydrate sources provide fiber. Fiber promotes fullness, supports a healthy colon, and prevents heart disease. While this may not sound like a direct benefit to your training, it translates to a healthier body for training. Good sources of fiber are fruits and vegetables as well as beans, whole grains, and tubers (e.g., white potatoes, yams). As a general rule, adults should consume 25 to 40 grams of fiber; the lower end of that range is more ideal for women and the higher end is ideal for men.

In choosing sources of carbohydrate, be aware of the glycemic index. The glycemic index measures the impact of food on blood sugar level. The closer to 100 a food is on the glycemic index, the more drastic of an effect it can have on boosting blood sugar levels. Foods with a glycemic index of 70 or more are considered high glycemic (HGI), while those with 55 or less are low glycemic (LGI). Table 4.1 lists the glycemic index ranges of common foods.

Traditionally, athletes have been told to eat sources of low-glycemic carbohydrate before a long training session or competition (lasting at least 90 minutes) so as to avoid any significant spikes in blood glucose levels, which may affect energy and thus performance. However, there is not enough research to show that consuming low glycemic–index carbohydrate before an endurance event contributes to superior performance (instead of eating foods higher on the glycemic index). The results may vary according to individual. More important, as athletes, the priority should be to focus on consuming whole sources of carbohydrate rather than processed alternatives.

Table 4.1 Glycemic Index of Common Foods

	Low GI (1–55)	Medium GI (56–69)	High GI (70–100)
Low GL (1–10)	All-bran cereal 8/38 Apple 6/38 Carrots 2/39 Chickpeas 8/28 Lentils 5/29 Grapes 8/46 Kidney beans 6/22 Orange 4/40 Pinto beans 8/33 Strawberries 1/40 Sweet corn 9/52 Peanuts 1/14 Milk, skim 5/37 Milk, full fat 5/41 Oatmeal cookies 10/55 Peanut M&M's 5/33 Honey 10/55	Pineapple 7/59 Cantaloupe 4/65 Popcorn 7/65 Wheat crackers 9/67 Yogurt, sweetened 3/66 Ice cream, regular 8/61 Couscous 9/65	Waffle 10/76 Watermelon 4/72 White or wheat bread 10/70 Whole wheat bread 9/71
Medium GL (11–19)	Apple juice 11/40 Orange juice 12/50 Milk, chocolate 12/43 Banana 11/47 Spaghetti, whole wheat 15/37 Fettuccine 18/40 Rice, white 14/38 Rice, brown 16/50 Sourdough wheat bread 15/54 Chocolate 12/43 Banana cake 18/47 Ensure 16/48 Frozen yogurt 11/51 Potato chips 11/54	Raisin Bran 12/61 Oatmeal, instant 17/66 Corn chips 17/63 Angel food cake 19/67 Cola soft drinks 16/63 Bran muffin 14/60 Honey 12/61	Cheerios 15/74 Grape Nut Flakes 17/80 Shredded Wheat 15/75 Potatoes, mashed 14/74 Potatoes, instant 17/85 Gatorade 12/78 Rice cakes 17/82 Graham crackers 14/74 Pretzels 16/83 Vitasoy rice milk 17/79
High GL (20+)	Long-grain wild rice 21/49 Vanilla cake with vanilla frosting 24/42 Chocolate cake with chocolate frosting 20/38	Raisins 28/64 Bagel, white 24/69 PowerBar 24/58 Clif Bar 22/57 Mixed fruit, dried 24/60 Rice, instant 28/69 Spaghetti, white 27/61 Pancakes 38/67 French fries 21/64	Potatoes, baked 26/85 Sweet potato 22/70 Cornflakes 20/81 Rice Krispies 21/82 French fries 22/75 Fig fruit bars 21/70 Pop-Tarts 25/70 Jelly beans 22/78

The first number listed is glycemic load (GL); the second number is glycemic index (GI).
Foods with higher glycemic values produce a faster rise in blood sugar (glucose) than do foods with lower values. Nothing produces a faster rise in blood glucose than pure glucose, which has a glycemic index of 100. A slow, steady rise in blood glucose is generally better tolerated than a sudden rise in blood glucose. Foods with a glycemic index below 70, therefore, are preferable for usual consumption.

Reprinted, by permission, from S.G. Eberle, 2014, *Endurance sports nutrition*, 3rd ed. (Champaign, IL: Human Kinetics), 85.

The following foods are good sources of healthy carbohydrate:

Whole grains, including amaranth, barley, corn, oats, quinoa, millet, rye, wheat, and rice

Potatoes, yams, and other tubers

Fruits

Vegetables

Low-fat milk and yogurt

During a longer training session or event (exceeding 90 minutes), you may need a quick burst of energy offered by energy gels, blocks, and similar products, which are often high in sugar and other refined carbohydrate. Try to limit your intake of processed simple carbohydrate to these instances.

Protein

Like carbohydrate, protein provides energy, but its primary function is to build, maintain, and repair body tissue. You'll need to consume enough protein in order to promote muscular development and recovery from your training. Each gram of protein contains 4 calories. Protein is made up of amino acids, which not only help with maintaining and building body tissue but also support other functions including the absorption of vitamins and minerals.

In total, there are 20 amino acids your body needs: 9 are essential amino acids and 11 are nonessential. The essential amino acids are not produced by the body and need to be obtained by food. These are some of the more nutrient-dense sources of essential amino acids:

Lean meats

Fish

Legumes

Nuts

Seeds

Soy and tofu

Eggs

You need to consume a variety of protein sources to ensure you are taking in all the amino acids your body needs.

You might be familiar with high-protein, low-carbohydrate diets for weight loss. Although these diets may help with weight-loss goals, they can be detrimental to sport performance. Your body needs enough carbohydrate to fuel performance, particularly anaerobic activity. Diets low in carbohydrate often mean your body will have to dip into protein for energy. On the other hand, it's still important to ensure you are eating enough protein to support muscle repair and recovery. For athletes, the general recommendation is to get 20 to 30 percent of your total daily calories from protein.

Be aware of some of the warning signs of a protein-deficient eating plan. Thinning hair, brittle nails, sleeplessness, brain fog, weakness, and longer recovery after workouts are all symptoms of insufficient protein intake. Be sure to eat enough protein to avoid these symptoms.

On the other hand, it's also possible to eat too much protein, particularly at the expense of not consuming enough carbohydrate. Like any other macronutrient your body doesn't use, protein can be stored as energy, which can lead to weight gain. And if you consume fatty cuts of meat or other protein sources higher in fat, you may be at risk of elevating your cholesterol level. Also, if you don't drink enough water, excess protein can compound dehydration as your kidneys work to filter out and flush the nitrogen in protein. Overall, listen to your body; drink enough water (which we'll get into later); and try to focus your protein intake on lean, low-fat sources.

Fat

Fat contains the greatest amount of energy content of all three macronutrients. One gram of fat has 9 calories, more than twice that of carbohydrate and protein. Fat supports the body with energy storage, insulation and protection of internal organs, cell membrane formation, brain functioning, and hormone production.

While fat has been demonized for years because of its high caloric content, in recent years the benefits of "good fat" have been highly touted. Unsaturated fats, which are liquid at room temperature, are good types of fat and include monounsaturated and polyunsaturated. Sources of monounsaturated fat are nuts, vegetable oil, olive oil, sunflower oil, and avocado. Polyunsaturated fat contains omega-3 and -6 fatty acids; sources are soybean oil, corn oil, and safflower oil. Flax and chia seeds as well as certain types of fish such as salmon, tuna, and trout also contain omega-3 fatty acids.

On the other end of the spectrum, saturated fat and hydrogenated (or trans) fat are solid at room temperature and are typically high in cholesterol. Foods high in saturated fat are full-fat cheese and milk, high-fat cuts of meat, ice cream, butter, and palm kernel oil. Fried foods and baked goods made from shortening are some of the richest sources of trans fat. As much as possible, avoid hydrogenated (trans) fat. Both saturated and trans fats may increase risk of cardiovascular disease.

Aim to consume 15 to 20 percent of your total daily calories from fat (or 1 to 2 grams of fat per kilogram of body weight). In general, it's best to consume the bulk of your fat calories from unsaturated fat sources and limit saturated fat intake to no more than 10 percent of your total daily calories. If you're not eating enough fat, you may exhibit symptoms of a fat-deficient diet that include hunger, mental fatigue, coldness due to your body's inability to regulate internal temperature, dry skin, limited absorption of vitamins and minerals, and increased risk of certain cancers (because omega-3 fatty acids help with prevention of colon, breast, and prostate cancers).

FAT-ADAPTED ATHLETES

Recently, a new diet trend has emerged in the circles of endurance athletes. The fat-adapted diet focuses on consumption of healthy fat, rather than carbohydrate, in order to meet energy needs. Anecdotally, these high-fat, low-carbohydrate diets have shown some benefits for endurance performance as well as weight loss. Whether or not the same benefits carry over to obstacle athletes remains to be seen because the research on high-fat, low-carbohydrate diets is limited and focused on highly trained endurance athletes.

As a general rule, a diet higher in carbohydrate and low in fat is recommended for athletes during the in-season. Training the body to depend on fat for energy takes time and know-how and should not be pursued less than a few months leading up to an event. Also, while a fat-adapted diet has helped fit endurance athletes with improve aerobic capacity and fitness, the impact of these diets on anaerobic performance has not been established.

Vitamins and Minerals

Unlike carbohydrate, protein, and fat, vitamins and minerals are micronutrients needed in small amounts. Vitamins and minerals help with growth, development, metabolism, and other functions. Vitamins are organic substances, while some minerals are organic (i.e., bound to organic molecules). Table 4.2 lists some of the vitamins and minerals your body needs along with food sources that contain them. Many vitamins and minerals are essential, and to ensure you eat all you need, it's important to eat nutrient-dense foods. You could also take a daily multivitamin to fill in the gaps in your diet, but the priority should be to eat a healthy, balanced diet. Supplement if necessary.

It may be a challenge to consume enough vitamins in your diet. In particular, many athletes find it challenging to meet their daily dietary needs of iron and calcium, two minerals especially important to the athlete's diet. You'll need these minerals to help support your training. Iron aids in red blood cell formation, while calcium helps maintain bone density and development. In these cases, you may find it helpful to take a daily iron and calcium supplement. But before doing so, ensure your diet consists of sources rich in iron and calcium. Food sources of iron are beef, chicken liver, shellfish, sardines, breakfast cereals enriched with iron, beans, broccoli, and spinach. Calcium-rich foods are milk (cow and fortified soy or almond milk), cheese, yogurt, and dark leafy greens, including spinach, kale, and collard greens.

Table 4.2 Dietary Reference Intakes (DRI) for Vitamins and Minerals

Vitamin or mineral	Dietary reference intake (DRI) for females/males age 19 to 50	Best food sources	What it does
Thiamin	1.1/1.2 mg/d	Wheat germ, whole-grain breads and cereals, organ meats, lean meats, legumes, fortified grains	Releases energy from carbohydrate; maintains healthy nervous system
Riboflavin	1.1/1.3 mg/d	Milk and dairy products, green leafy vegetables, lean meats, beans, fortified grains	Releases energy from protein, fat, and carbohydrate; promotes healthy skin
Niacin	14/16 mg/d	Lean meats, fish, poultry, legumes, whole grains, fortified grains	Releases energy from protein, fat, and carbohydrate; aids in synthesis of protein, fat, and DNA; promotes healthy skin and nervous system
Vitamin B_6	1.3 mg/d	Liver, lean meats, fish, poultry, legumes, whole grains	Aids in metabolism of protein; synthesis of essential fatty acids; forms hemoglobin and red blood cells
Vitamin B_{12}	2.4 gm/d	Lean meats, poultry, dairy products, eggs, fish	Aids in metabolism of carbohydrate, protein, fat; produces red blood cells; maintains nerve cells
Folate	400 gm/d	Green leafy vegetables, legumes	Aids growth of new cells; forms red blood cells
Biotin	30 gm/d	Meats, legumes, milk, egg yolk, whole grains	Aids in metabolism of carbohydrate, fat, protein
Pantothenic acid	5 mg/d	Found in variety of foods	Aids in metabolism of carbohydrate, fat, protein

Vitamin or mineral	Dietary reference intake (DRI) for females/males age 19 to 50	Best food sources	What it does
Vitamin C	75/90 mg/d	Citrus fruits, green leafy vegetables, broccoli, peppers, potatoes, berries, kiwi, cantaloupe (rock melon)	Maintains normal connective tissue; enhances iron absorption; serves as antioxidant; helps heal wounds
Vitamin A	700/900 gm/d	Liver, milk, cheese, fortified margarine, carotenoids in plant foods (orange, red, or deep green in color)	Maintains healthy skin, mucous membranes, vision, and immune system; serves as antioxidant
Vitamin D	600 IU/d	Vitamin D–fortified milk and margarine, fattier fish, fish oil, sunlight	Promotes normal bone growth; aids in calcium absorption
Vitamin E	15 mg/d	Vegetable oils, margarine, green leafy vegetables, wheat germ, eggs, whole grains	Serves as antioxidant; helps to form red blood cells
Vitamin K	90/120 gm/d	Liver, eggs, cauliflower, green leafy vegetables	Promotes normal blood clotting
Calcium	1,000 mg/d	Milk, cheese, yogurt, ice cream, legumes, dark green leafy vegetables	Helps in formation of bones and teeth; has role in muscle contractions, nerve impulse transmission, and blood clotting
Phosphorus	700 mg/d	Meat, poultry, fish, eggs, milk, cheese, legumes, whole grains	Aids in metabolism of protein, carbohydrate, and fat; repairs and maintains cells; helps in formation of teeth and bones
Magnesium	320/420 mg/d	Milk, yogurt, legumes, nuts, whole grains, tofu, green vegetables	Aids in metabolism of carbohydrate and protein; aids in neuromuscular contractions
Iron	18/8 mg/d	Organ meats, lean meats, poultry, shellfish, oysters, whole grains, legumes	Aids in formation of hemoglobin and transportation of oxygen in red blood cells

(continued)

TABLE 4.2 (continued)

Vitamin or mineral	Dietary reference intake (DRI) for females/males age 19 to 50	Best food sources	What it does
Zinc	8/11 mg/d	Lean meats, fish, poultry, shellfish, oysters, whole grains, legumes	Aids in energy metabolism; synthesizes protein; helps with immune function and wound healing
Copper	900 gm/d	Lean meats, poultry, shellfish, fish, eggs, nuts, beans, whole grains	Is necessary for iron absorption, manufacture of collagen; heals wounds
Fluoride	3/4 mg/d	Milk, egg yolks, water, seafood	Helps form teeth and bones
Selenium	55 gm/d	Meat, fish, poultry, organ meats, seafood, whole grains, and nuts from selenium-rich soil	Serves as component of antioxidant enzymes
Chromium	25/35 gm/d	Organ meats, meats, oysters, cheese, whole grains, beer	Regulates blood sugar; aids normal fat metabolism
Iodine	150 gm/d	Iodized salt, seafood, water	Serves as component of thyroid hormone that helps regulate growth and development rate
Manganese	1.8/2.3 mg/d	Green leafy vegetables, whole grains, nuts, legumes, egg yolks	Aids in synthesis of hemoglobin
Molybdenum	45 gm/d	Legumes, cereal grains, dark green leafy vegetables	Involved in carbohydrate and fat metabolism
Sodium	Daily need varies based on sweat losses, at least 1,500 mg/d	Table salt; found in virtually all foods, especially processed items	Promotes acid–base balance, fluid balance, nerve impulses, muscle action
Potassium	4,700 mg/d; if high sweat rate, may need more	Fruits and vegetables (bananas, orange juice, potatoes, tomatoes), milk, yogurt, legumes	Promotes fluid balance, acid–base balance, nerve impulses, muscle action, synthesis of protein and glycogen

Note: mg = microgram; gm = gram; /d = day

DRI listed for males (M) is for men ages 19 to 50; females (F) is for nonpregnant women ages 19 to 50.

Reprinted, by permission, from S.G. Eberle, 2014, *Endurance sports nutrition*, 3rd ed. (Champaign, IL: Human Kinetics), 87.

Water

Although water does not fit into the category of macro- or micronutrients, it's an important nutrient that deserves mention. Water supports bodily processes such as temperature regulation, nutrient transport, and digestive regularity. You actually need to consume more water than any other nutrient. Although a commonly cited recommendation is 8 cups of water a day (64 oz, or 2 L), athletes need more to replace water loss through exercise. Try to drink 4 to 8 ounces (120-240 ml) of water every 15 to 30 minutes during exercise and continue hydrating afterward.

There are several ways your body lets you know if you need more water. First, you can tell by the color your urine; it should be light in color and clear, but if it's dark yellow or orange, that's an indication that you're dehydrated. Other indications of dehydration can be noted by the way you feel as you train and race. Water loss of 1.5 percent of your body weight can interfere with performance. Dehydration can lead to impaired cognitive performance, slow movement, decreased running pace, decline in precision, and feelings of fatigue and faintness. Sometimes athletes, particularly bodybuilders and fitness competitors, cut out water and water-retaining foods in order to lose weight. As obstacle athletes, this is not a good idea, based on the effects of dehydration.

In extreme temperatures—particularly hot, humid weather—staying hydrated is especially critical. If you are training or racing during the summer months or in a hot and humid area, you will need 4 to 8 ounces (120-240 ml) of water every 15 to 30 minutes. Don't wait until you are thirsty to hydrate, because thirst is a preliminary symptom of dehydration, which you will especially want to avoid in hot, humid weather. And for workouts and races lasting more than an hour, you may need a sport drink to replenish electrolyte loss. Even if you think you are sufficiently hydrating, be aware of the warning signs of heat related-illnesses. Feelings of fatigue, clamminess, stickiness (indicating that your sweat is not evaporating off your skin), loss of coordination, and dizziness are all signs of extreme dehydration, which can lead to heat cramps, heat exhaustion, heatstroke, and in rare cases death. Gradually work up to training and racing in hot weather because your body will need time to acclimate.

Nutrition Guidelines for Obstacle Athletes

Beyond nutrition basics, there are other considerations you need to keep in mind. First, how many calories are enough to fuel your training and other energy requirements on a daily basis? Second, are there any supplements beyond a multivitamin you should consider? And how do any special dietary concerns affect your eating plan?

OBSTACLE RACING AND ALCOHOL

Enjoying a postrace beer is a trademark in obstacle races. It's part of the culture. You've finished the course, so why not celebrate with friends afterward? Race organizers often provide a free beer (or two) for participants.

But what impact does alcohol have on your training and health? A gram of alcohol contains 7 calories, which is more energy per gram than carbohydrate or protein. Not all alcohol is created equal. Some types are higher in sugar content than others, which, after a race, may not matter as much as during your training. Beer is higher in sugar content than wine and most hard liquors, excluding cocktails.

While in training, excessive alcohol consumption can hinder your hard work. It can interfere with memory retention, learning new skills, and sleep cycles. As a diuretic, it can also speed up water loss. However, in moderation, consumption may help with recovery because it can help your body and muscles relax.

Various opinions exist on recommendations of alcohol consumption during training and the impact of alcohol on athletes. In general, moderate consumption is okay during training, but it would be wise to refrain from drinking alcohol the day and hours leading to your race so you don't risk sabotaging performance.

Fueling Goals and Competition Needs

Your caloric intake will vary depending on where you are in your season. An athlete in season will have a different eating plan from an athlete in the off-season trying to lose a bit of weight or build muscle. If you're in season with a planned stretch of events over a few months or just weeks away from your race, you need to focus on eating enough to fuel your workouts and recovery from training. It's not time to cut back because low-calorie diets may hamper your performance. In addition to eating enough for training purposes, you'll need to account for your other daily activities. Table 4.3 shows estimated daily caloric needs for male and female athletes based on training goals and other levels of activity.

In your off-season, you can work on weight loss or muscle gain if fine-tuning your body composition is a goal. Although restricting calories is a common way to aid in weight loss, be conscious of cutting back too much. Your body will let you know when you're not taking in

Table 4.3 Estimated Daily Caloric Needs for Male and Female Athletes

Activity level	Examples of activity level	Examples of athletes	Estimated daily caloric need (kcal/kg)	
			Females	Males
Sedentary (little physical activity)	Sitting or standing with little activity (e.g., desk or computer work, light housekeeping, TV, video games)	During recovery from injury	30	31
Moderate-intensity exercise 3-5 days/week or low-intensity and short-duration training daily	Playing recreational tennis (singles) 1-1.5 hours every other day Practicing baseball, softball, or golf 2.5 hours 5 days/week	Baseball players Softball players Golfers Recreational tennis players	35	38
Training several hours daily, 5 days/week	Swimming 6,000-10,000 meters/day plus some resistance training Conditioning and skills training 2-3 hours/day	Swimmers Soccer players	37	41
Rigorous training on a near-daily basis	Resistance exercise 10-15 hours/week to maintain well-developed muscle mass Swimming 7,000-17,000 meters/day and resistance training 3 days/week	Bodybuilders (maintenance phase) College and professional basketball and American football players Elite swimmers Rugby players	38-40	45
	Training for a triathlon	Nonelite triathletes	41	51.5
Extremely rigorous training	Running 15 miles (24 km)/day or equivalent	Elite runners, distance cyclists, triathletes	50 or more	60 or more

Reprinted, by permission, from M. Macedonio and M. Dunford, 2009, *Athlete's guide to making weight* (Champaign, IL: Human Kinetics), 82.

enough. Signs of extremely low-calorie diets include irritability, fatigue, moodiness, and sleeplessness. Cutting more than 20 percent of your daily caloric needs will often lead to these symptoms. One pound (0.45 kg) of fat is roughly 3,500 calories, which means that if you cut back about 100 to 150 calories a day, you can lose about a pound a month; cut back 200 to 300 calories and you may lose a couple pounds a month. Some extreme diet plans cut back as much as 1,000 calories a day, which may lead to 2 pounds or more of weight loss a week; however, this is too drastic for athletes.

For muscle gain, you'll need to adjust your caloric intake. Building mass and muscle requires you to consume your daily caloric needs while training for strength and muscular development balanced with cardiorespiratory exercise to maintain fitness. The general recommendation is to add 300 to 500 calories per day to your baseline. Men may add up to 500 calories, while women may need only an additional 300 daily calories. You may engage in some trial and error to see how your body responds.

Sometimes your goal in the off-season may be to simply stay in shape for obstacle racing or perhaps improve on a specific aspect of fitness such as your running pace or strength. In this case, cutting back on calories is not necessary. Be sure you eat enough to fuel the hard work you'll put into supporting your health and performance goals. Overall, if you have any questions or need more guidance, find a board-registered dietitian or nutritionist through the Academy of Nutrition and Dietetics, or consult with your doctor.

Supplementation

Even with a balanced, healthy diet, you may want to consider supplementation to help promote overall health and support performance goals. Aside from a multivitamin, some athletes consider taking branched-chain amino acids (BCAAs) or a joint support supplement.

Three of the 20 amino acids are BCAAs: leucine, isoleucine, and valine. BCAAs may help reduce breakdown of muscle, delay muscle fatigue during exercise, and assist with muscle recovery after exercise. Athletes who engage in regular strength training sometimes take BCAA supplements. Unless you are in your off-season working on building muscle, you probably take in enough BCAA through your diet. BCAAs are in meat, whey, eggs, and dairy products. Vegan sources of BCAAs are soybeans, lentils, baked beans, lima beans, chickpeas, almonds, cashews, hemp seeds, Brazil nuts, and sesame seeds.

Another supplement option is a joint support formula, which is especially relevant to athletes and exercisers who engage in high-impact activity. The content of joint support supplements may vary across manufacturers, but most contain glucosamine and chondroitin. Often used to ease mild arthritis, glucosamine and chondroitin help maintain healthy cartilage and joints. Glucosamine and chondroitin levels in cartilage decrease with age, so sometimes supplementation is helpful, especially for older athletes. Since most joint support formulas are made up of glucosamine and chondroitin derived from shark and other fish cartilage, this supplement may not be an option for vegetarians and vegans. Alternatively, some studies have shown that plant-based sources of omega-3, particularly flaxseed oil, may help support joint health.

Special Diets

If you have a special diet, how is your eating plan for performance affected? This will vary depending on your dietary restrictions. If you have diabetes, high blood pressure, gluten intolerance, or other special concerns, it's best to consult with a board-registered dietitian or nutritionist for guidance that is specific to your needs.

If you are vegetarian or vegan, your daily nutrition needs remain the same as those of omnivore athletes. It's a common misconception that vegetarian and vegan athletes need to consume more protein than their omnivore counterparts. However, there are many plant-based sources of protein and ways to combine various plant-based protein sources in order to ensure protein needs are met. Plant-based sources of protein are soybeans, tofu, tempeh, mycoprotein, beans, lentils, quinoa, and nuts, including nut butters.

Pre- and Postrace Nutrition

Nutrition is a significant factor in race-day performance. Race-day nutrition doesn't just refer to solid foods you eat; it has to do with hydration and electrolyte supplementation as well. In the remainder of this chapter we review solid foods, hydration, and supplementation needs for your race.

What you eat right before your race is important, but eating consistently well all week leading up to a race is the best way to prepare yourself for a high-quality performance. While some athletes consider carb loading before a race (eating one or two more servings than usual of carbohydrate foods a few days before a race), we place greater emphasis on getting your body used to a healthy eating routine. It is important that you provide your body with appropriate fuel all week long and not introduce your digestive system to anything that might upset it. Stick to lean meats throughout the week (or nonmeat protein for vegetarians and vegans), grains such as quinoa and rice, and lots of fruits and vegetables.

Do your best over the course of the week to hydrate appropriately as well. Hydration comes down to two major components: fluids and electrolytes. Electrolyte usage is particularly important for longer challenges, the prerace period, and during the event itself. You need to be hydrated at both a cellular level and a blood plasma level. The proper adjustment in hydration varies per person, but most athletes need to take in more fluids in preparation for a longer race. However, if this is something your body is not used to, you may run into problems both with electrolyte balance and in terms of gastrointestinal regularity.

Gastrointestinal distress can be a result of increased water consumption. Most notably, this can manifest itself as diarrhea. Many endurance athletes face this issue as they deal with the increased amounts of fluids traveling through the intestines. You should get your body used to heightened fluid consumption by gradually raising your fluid intake over a few weeks. Once adjusted to your elevated daily hydration levels, you'll find your system will begin to function as normal. Be warned that it can often take a couple weeks to reach this stage.

Race-Day Nutrition

So, you've made it to race day and you need some tips on eating and fueling to maximize your race performance. You've eaten well and hydrated properly all week, which certainly make things much easier. The first thing you should do when you wake up is take in your calories for the morning. You want ample time to digest so your cells can be fueled and so your stomach is not upset. And let's be honest: You want to have to go to the bathroom *before* the race, not during. Wake up at least 2.5 hours before your event to eat breakfast, take in some fluids, and digest.

You could ask 100 athletes what to eat in the morning and they could give you 100 different answers. It is important to consume a reasonable amount of fat, carbohydrate, and protein in your prerace meal. And make sure that it is something your body is used to; don't throw your digestive system a curveball on race day.

There's an unwritten rule that most experienced racers adhere to: Never change anything on race day. That goes for the clothes you wear, the way you hydrate, and, most important, the way you eat. You must be accustomed to eating and digesting everything you put into your body on race day.

The best thing you can do is keep it simple. Half of a bagel with peanut butter and jelly can provide all of the fat and simple and complex carbohydrate your body needs for an event, as can a banana dipped in honey and some avocado. Many swear by a bowl of oatmeal and fruit. Whatever you choose to eat in the morning, make sure you put high-quality foods into your body for race day that your body is accustomed to digesting.

Many also regularly ask about the value of coffee on race days. Keep in mind that coffee can affect your body in many ways. Coffee gets your digestive system moving in the morning. Be sure to drink it early enough so that your digestive system isn't functioning in overdrive at the start of the race. Coffee can certainly help you clear out your system before the event, but that's not its only benefit.

The caffeine in coffee can improve performance by providing energy. It is also believed to be able to numb your muscle receptors to pain and fatigue and allow you to push on. Although the impact of caffeine may differ among athletes, caffeine can boost performance, particularly in sports that tap into endurance, like obstacle racing.

However, it's important to use caffeine with caution. Some believe that caffeine before exercise can lead to increased dehydration because it is a diuretic and may raise your internal body temperature. It can also make you jittery if you consume too much and can cause an upset stomach if consumed in high quantities, none of which you want on race day. Generally, one or two cups of coffee should not hurt your race performance, so feel free to have a cup or two on the morning of your race without fear if you're used to it. Above all, be mindful of your body's response to caffeine intake. Sometimes the best measure to take on race day is to keep your caffeine intake the same as usual for you; overdoing it on race day may increase your likelihood of experiencing the more inconvenient effects of caffeine.

In-Race Fueling

You're now standing on the starting line. You ate a high-quality breakfast. You're hydrated. And now you must run your race, fueling along the way. Items you may need include energy gels, electrolyte tablets, and possibly even a hydration pack (as mentioned in chapter 3).

Many athletes like to have a jolt of energy to kick off a race, so they consume an energy gel at the starting line while waiting for the race to begin. Please note that when doing so, you will want to consume at least 8 ounces of water with the gel. Energy gels typically need water in order to function, so they will pull the water from your body if you do not wash the gel down with enough fluid. Throughout your race, it is recommended you consume an energy gel about every 45 minutes, even more frequently in very long or taxing events. Plan accordingly and have the appropriate gear to carry those gels.

It is also recommended you take an electrolyte tablet or two on the starting line as well as every 45 minutes or so. This will help you maintain an appropriate chemical balance and allow you to maintain proper hydration levels as well as you continue to sweat during your race. If swallowing pills during a run is not your thing, a variety of less potent options disintegrate in water. You simply drop it in your water and drink—problem solved!

Use all of the water stops available to you. Unless you are a pro racer in a short race, the additional water will prove essential over the course of a race that takes numerous hours to complete, particularly if you are consuming gels and electrolyte tablets along the way. And if you aren't carrying fluids, skipping those water stations can have fairly unfortunate results.

However, if you fuel appropriately and hydrate correctly, your results in your first event will be determined by how well you prepared your body during training. And in the following chapters, you will learn to do that incredibly well.

Postrace Nutrition

After the race, your body will be in need of a lot of care. Obviously, you'll have bumps, bruises, and scrapes, maybe even a little swelling in your joints. But, in reality, that's mostly superficial. What about all of the needs your body has inside, at a cellular level?

You just ran a race that required you to prepare for months, eat well, hydrate appropriately, and take electrolytes just to get through it. Well, shouldn't it stand to reason that your postrace nutrition needs to be on point to allow your body to recover as quickly as possible? Of course it does. Your body will be dehydrated, your muscle fibers damaged, and your glycogen stores low.

First, hydrate. As soon as you cross that finish line, you need to begin taking in fluids. Your system will be depleted and you will need to consume water throughout the day and possibly continue your electrolyte consumption as well. As you know by now, hydration is a two-part process: fluids and electrolytes. You most likely won't be able to fully hydrate again at both blood plasma and cellular levels in just a day of fluid intake, so most likely you'll need to up your intake for a few days after your race.

Second, be sure to consume protein (ideally in the form of liquid) within the first 45 minutes of finishing the race in order to begin the muscle repair process. Bars can be useful, but it is recommended to opt for the two old reliable options: whey and casein protein powder.

Whey and casein protein are both found in milk. Whey is considered fast acting because the small molecules it is composed of are ideal for quick absorption into the body. Whey is the ideal postworkout or postrace protein. Casein, on the other hand, is slow acting, a larger-molecule protein that absorbs much more slowly into the system than whey does. Casein protein is the second piece of the puzzle for muscle repair. Casein is best consumed at night before bedtime, providing your body with a steady source of protein to fuel muscle repair for hours as you sleep.

Keep a small packet or sealable plastic bag of protein powder and a shaker in your bag so you can quickly make yourself a postrace shake and kick-start your recovery process quickly and on the cheap. There's no point in waiting to drink a shake. All it will do is delay your recovery process, and your goal is to bounce back as quickly as possible. As you may already know, some athletes can attest to the benefits of chocolate milk as a recovery drink after a strenuous workout or challenging event. If you are a regular-milk drinker and not lactose intolerant, chocolate milk after a hard race is an option to help your body recover and repair. (Be sure to reserve that chocolate milk drink for after your race because it contains a lot of sugar, which is ideal after a tough race, but not necessary after most of your workouts.)

Branched-chain amino acids (BCAAs) are also key to muscle repair. Most protein powders contain BCAAs, but it never hurts to check the label and make sure you're getting them with your protein supplement.

So now you've covered hydration and muscle repair postrace, but you may still find your energy levels are low. When you complete a taxing event, glycogen stores are often depleted and you need to refill them. Glycogen is the chemical form of carbohydrate that is stored in the muscles and liver.

The best way to reload is to introduce carbohydrate into your diet shortly after the completion of your event. Ideally, the carbohydrate can be mixed with the protein supplement. Many postworkout supplements even come already loaded with carbohydrate. Your ideal ratio of carbohydrate to protein is 3:1 to 4:1. Add that to your diet postrace, and ideally even postworkout, and you have a recipe for rapid recovery.

Based on our postrace guidelines, you may get the idea that some of the options at a race may not be the most nutritious options. The truth is that you won't always know what to expect, so it's a good idea to bring your own postrace fuel in case your options are limited. The occasional pizza or large sandwich after a race is okay, but if you have several races planned for the season, you'll want to feed your body what it craves in order to recover from a challenge. Some nutrition bars at races may fit the ideal carbohydrate-to-protein ratio of 3:1 or 4:1, so you can have those instead of a shake. Once you've had your postrace recovery snack, try to eat a healthy meal within a couple hours of your finish time; you'll be hungry for a meal soon afterward.

Final Thoughts

By now, you should be equipped with a basic knowledge of macronutrients, micronutrients, water, and alcohol. You should strive to consume 55 to 60 percent of your total calories from carbohydrate, 25 to 30 percent from protein, and 15 to 20 percent from fat. A diet rich in a variety of healthy food choices can help you meet your daily requirements for vitamins and minerals. You know you need to hydrate adequately. You also know how to calculate your caloric intake requirements, determine your supplementation needs, and consider special dietary restrictions. You've learned how to fuel specifically for your race-day needs. Keep these guidelines in mind as you prepare for the challenging workouts you'll discover in part III.

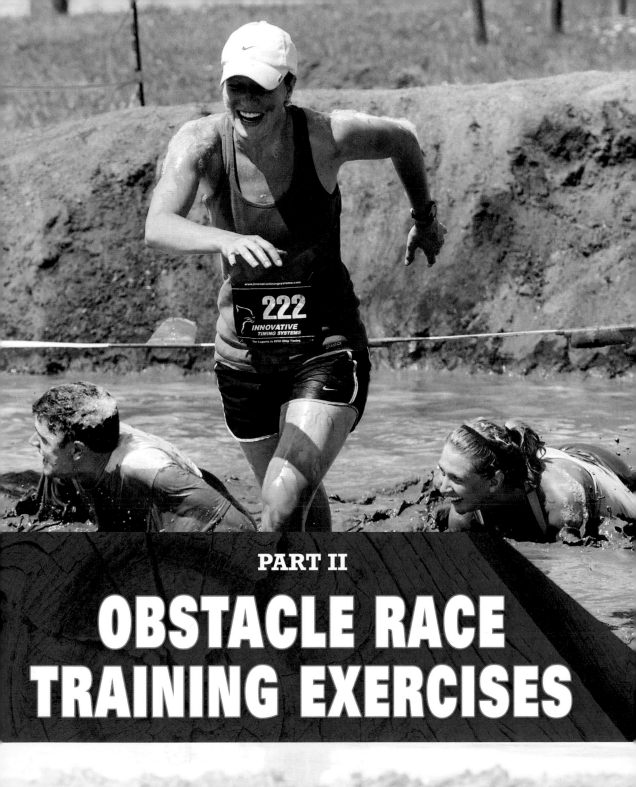

PART II

OBSTACLE RACE
TRAINING EXERCISES

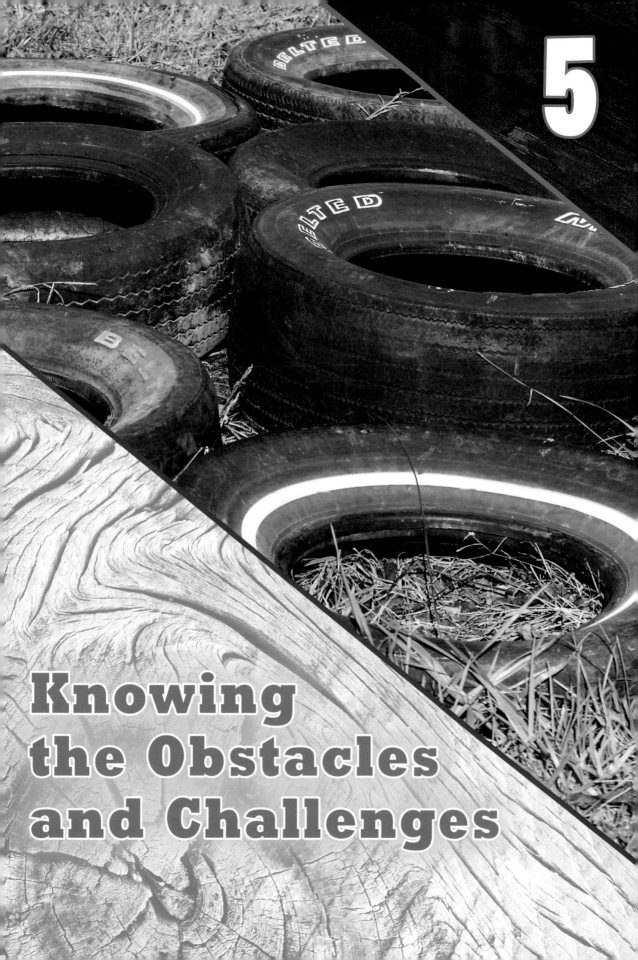

5

Knowing the Obstacles and Challenges

With his next race a few months away, Chris is determined to improve his performance with obstacles, especially the ones he simply could not do. Running, all by itself, has always been difficult for Chris, and he struggled with maintaining endurance during the race. He also couldn't get over the higher walls, and he could manage to get through only a few rungs on the monkey bars. Chris wants to know the ins and outs of each common obstacle and how to conquer them.

astering the obstacles themselves is probably the most enjoyable and relevant portion of prerace preparation. Learning to navigate them not just effectively but also efficiently is the key to a high-quality race. This chapter cannot encompass all challenges in a given race, and specific races have different demands. Many races are constantly evolving from year to year. In this chapter we describe a variety of obstacles and challenges that frequently appear in races, organized into the following categories: endurance (aerobic and muscular), mobility and balance, strength and power, grip strength, and mental strength. Keep in mind that during the course of an obstacle race, many of these demands overlap. For example, some obstacles like wall climbing require grip strength, mobility, and upper-body strength. Obstacle racing often integrates several demands over the course of a race, which you may have already learned firsthand. Let's start with endurance.

Endurance

Endurance is the greatest physical requirement in being prepared for an obstacle race. Endurance covers both aerobic capacity and muscular ability. Aerobic endurance taxes your cardiovascular and respiratory systems, while muscular endurance challenges the capacity of your muscular and skeletal systems to perform sustained work over time. Aerobic endurance covers activities like running—the main activity in obstacle racing—spread over the course of steep hills, muddy terrain, and a variety of other surface types. Muscular endurance covers sandbag, log, and bucket carries as well as tire and cinder-block drags.

Sometimes aerobic endurance and muscular endurance are worked at the same time in an obstacle race. For example, long periods of running, a swim across a stretch of water, or lifting a heavy object uphill will all tax your heart and lungs. However, these challenges will also call on your legs and arms, which need to be strong enough to get you through a long run, swim, or steep climb. Training to endure the accumulation of lactic acid in your muscles or to keep your feet moving after you've already been ascending an arduous course can be a challenge. Developing a high level of endurance can take months of consistent training and preparation.

Common Obstacles for Muscular Endurance

Sandbag Carry

The sandbag carry tests strength in picking up the sandbag, aerobic and muscular endurance in moving it, and mental fortitude in carrying a 20- to 60-pound (9-27 kg) bag on the shoulders up and down a large hill. Generally, these carries are not performed on flat ground unless the terrain is technical. The sandbag carry tests muscular endurance in the legs, specifically in the calves and quads, as well as spinal stability (lower-back strength). Many participants find their ability to run fast is zapped by a difficult sandbag carry and that their legs are more prone to cramps after the carry as well.

How to Conquer It

Set the bag evenly across your shoulders. Try not to lean too far forward, even as you go uphill. If you can, hold it with only one hand so you can pump your other arm to power your legs. That single-arm grip should be a reach across your body to the opposite shoulder, changing hands when your fingers tire.

Log Carry

Similar to the sandbag carry, the log carry challenges the same muscle groups but demands a bit more shoulder, biceps, and grip strength because the log lacks the flexibility of a sandbag and needs to be held more securely to the shoulder. Usually a log carry is up a hill and will test your pain threshold because the bark can be uncomfortable on your skin. Logs vary in size and weight but generally weigh 30 to 60 pounds (14-27 kg).

How to Conquer It

Set the log on one of your shoulders and grip it with the hand on that same side, leaving your other arm free to pump and keep your legs driving.

Bucket Carry

For many racers, the bucket carry can be a game changer—or their worst nightmare. The bucket carry requires you to fill a 5-gallon (20 L) bucket with rocks, water, or sand up to a fill line, then carry it around a loop. The bucket carry tends to challenge your body a bit differently than a log carry or sandbag carry because you need to hold it in front of you, above your hips. The bucket carry places a tremendous amount of strain on the spinal erectors (muscles in your lower back) as well as your grip strength and biceps muscles as you work to hold the bucket stable.

How to Conquer It

The grip is critical here. Holding the bottom with both hands will quickly wear out your grip strength. Instead, opt to wrap your arms around the bucket, pinning it high up against your chest. Place the fingers of one hand under the bucket and clasp that wrist with the opposite hand. That will take the weight off your fingers.

Cinder-Block Drag

Cinder-block drag refers to any kind of heavy drag. A large cinder block attached to a rope or chain functions as a strength–power obstacle. You pull the block, which weighs about 50 pounds (22 kg), around a track.

How to Conquer It

Instead of dragging the rope or chain behind you, pull it toward one side and over your hip. Keeping the front of the cinder block up will allow you to pull it more easily because it won't dig into the ground and resist you as much.

Weighted Drag

You might encounter two types of drags. The first is similar to the cinder-block drag, which involves pulling a car tire or sled behind you. The more challenging obstacle involves a cinder-block/large truck tire, sled, or weights tied to a rope. The other end of the rope is fastened to a stake in the ground. You pull the tire to the stake, generating leverage by bracing yourself with the stake. The pull uses strength in the quads and upper and lower back as well as biceps and grip. You must then grab the tire and drag it until the rope is taut again and ready for the next competitor.

How to Conquer It

Plant your feet against the stake and reach out far forward on the rope so you can make longer pulls. Drive through your heels while simultaneously leaning back and pulling the rope in toward your chest. The longer your pulls, the more ground you can cover on each pull. To drag the tire back, don't grab the tire itself; instead, grab the rope about 3 feet (1 m) in front of the tire. Run, dragging the rope along your hip, similar to the cinder-block drag. You'll save time and energy this way.

Mobility and Balance

Mobility and balance are integral pieces in an obstacle racer's tool kit. Think about all of the ways you might exhibit balance and mobility over the course of a race. You may need to navigate a series of logs or a wobbly balance beam without slipping. You'll need to be agile enough to roll under the gap in a wall immediately after scaling over one. You'll need hip and shoulder mobility so you can crawl under barbed wire uphill while circumventing logs and bales of hay. You'll need to use dynamic flexibility, coordination, core stability, and mechanics in order to land lightly on your feet. And you'll need to be able to do all this without letting it disrupt your rhythm once you return to running.

Common Obstacles for Mobility and Balance

Vertical Log Balance

While this obstacle has a variety of names, it is essentially a row of logs buried vertically in the ground. Generally the heights are about 2 to 3 feet high (0.6-1 m), the width of each log is generally 4 to 6 inches (10-15 cm), and the logs are usually spaced 3 to 5 feet (1-1.5 m). Logs might have varying heights, might not be aligned entirely straight, and might be very slippery. The objective of the obstacle is to walk from one end to the other without touching the ground. The log hop will challenge your balance, agility, and coordination.

How to Conquer It

Choose the path of least resistance. Aim for a row of logs of level height. Make sure the soles of your shoes aren't too wet. Try to stay relaxed, walking on the logs normally. Don't overthink it. Just walk on your toes.

Balance Beam

You might encounter several types of balance beams during races. It might be a beam a few inches wide and placed above water that you need to cross. Or it could be wobbly or loose, having some give as it shifts slightly side to side. A crude and often-used balance beam may simply be downed trees over a ditch that you're expected to run across. Or a twist on the balance beam may be a series of beams with sharp, angled corners and turns that require participants to change direction while maintaining balance.

How to Conquer It

Hold your arms out at your sides for balance. Hesitation is the enemy. Momentum is your friend—just as with riding a bike. Don't stop moving forward. You stand a better chance of completing the obstacle if you keep moving at a steady pace.

Low Crawl

The low crawl comes in a variety of setups. Most common is the barbed-wire crawl, where participants are expected to navigate 10 to 100 yards of the course while staying close to the ground. Sometimes you will be expected to navigate underneath a similar course, but instead of barbed wire, you will need to crawl beneath a series of wooden beams. And occasionally these crawls are tunnels or angled uphill.

How to Conquer It

In addition to staying low and crawling, when possible, roll sideways. It will move you faster and save energy.

Over-Under Obstacle

Another common obstacle requiring mobility, the over–under challenges participants to hop over a beam or wall and then immediately under another wall or net, often in a series of numerous overs and unders. (IMAGE). Sometimes there is a through portion to this obstacle, where participants are challenged to climb through a small opening in a wall.

How to Conquer It

To go over walls, get your chest over the wall and then swing your legs over, using momentum. You can almost slingshot your legs over the walls this way. To go under the walls, drop down and roll.

Grip Strength

Many people train to be strong and fast and develop great aerobic endurance, but they leave out an important element of fitness: grip strength. What good are big muscles if your fingers aren't strong enough to hang on to the monkey bars? Or hold on to a rope that is slick from the wet mud? While your back and biceps may be strong enough to navigate a wall or rope traverse, if you lack strength in your fingers or forearms, you won't have the ability to hang on and complete the obstacle. Preparing your hands and fingers to have not only strength and power but also the muscular endurance to function at the end of a race is critical to success.

Common Obstacles for Grip Strength

Monkey Bars

You climbed them countless times as a child. When we talk about obstacle racing making you feel like a kid again, the monkey bars are near the top of the list of challenges that fit that description. The monkey bars require you to swing from one bar to the next, sometimes as the height goes up and down. The bars and your hands may be caked with mud and slippery from water, depending on the obstacles you completed right before you got to the monkey bars. Often the bars have varying widths designed to challenge your grip as well as your shoulder mobility and stability.

How to Conquer It

If you have doubts about your grip strength, reverse your grip on your lead hand so your palms face inward toward one another. It will provide some added stability. Also, reach for only one rung at a time; don't try to skip rungs unless you're very confident in your abilities. It's slower but safer.

Rope Climb

The rope climb might have been a gym-class nightmare in your younger years. Requiring strength in your back and biceps muscles, the rope climb is made more difficult when it's slick with water and mud. If you lack proper form or strength, this obstacle can place a great deal of stress on your hands. The rope climb usually requires competitors to climb out of waist-deep water and ring a bell near the top or reach a similar object.

How to Conquer It

Pinch the rope between your knees and between your feet to take the pressure off your hands. Additionally, you can use a method like the J-hook or S-hook to make it easier on your hands. Leaning back to kick the bell is one way to get to the bell sooner and save your upper body from the additional stresses of climbing higher.

Wall Traverse

Wall traverses can come in several forms, but essentially the idea is to work your way from one end of the wall to the other using the handholds (and possibly footholds). Sometimes the grips are cut from 2-by-4 blocks of wood, or they might consist of handles, chains, or rock-climbing holds. Regardless, these obstacles will test not just your grip strength but also your coordination and hip mobility.

How to Conquer It

Keep your hips close to the wall and maintain three points of contact at all times. That means either two hands and one foot on the holds or one hand and two feet. Never remove both hands or both feet simultaneously from the holds.

Rope Traverse

An obstacle that's become more common lately and is considered one of the more difficult to master is the rope traverse. This traverse requires you to shimmy across a horizontal rope or cable without touching the ground. Often this obstacle is located over water in order to ensure you don't injure yourself when you fall.

How to Conquer It

There are two ways to get across this rope: above and below the rope. If you go above the rope, lie on top of the rope so that it runs between your legs, wrapping your foot up and over the rope. Reach out far in front and pull the rope to drag yourself forward. If you go below the rope, hang from your hands. Walk your feet one step at a time over the top of the rope, using your heels to hold you stable. The foot that steps should be opposite of the hand that moves so that you basically spider-walk across the rope. Never stop moving. That will only make you more tired, which will end badly.

The rope traverse challenges your strength in several ways, depending on how you navigate it. If you decide to cross headfirst, hanging underneath the rope from your hands and feet, you will find your grip strength is tremendously challenged, as is the strength in your shoulders, biceps, and back. The strength and flexibility in your groin and hamstring areas can be challenged by this motion as well as an internal rotation of the foot that is required for working your way across the rope.

If you opt to cross the rope on top, your biceps and back muscles will still be taxed, but your grip strength will in part be spared. You will, however, move more slowly than you would if you crossed the rope from underneath.

Hoist Obstacle

An obstacle that fits somewhere between grip strength and strength and power is the hoist obstacle. While there may be variations regarding how it is built, the obstacle is essentially a heavy weight attached to a rope that runs through a pulley. Competitors must grab the rope, pull the rope down, and get the weight all the way to the top. Often this rope is wet, muddy, and slippery. The weight can sometimes be so heavy that it lifts competitors off the ground. Sometimes that weight is made of stone or cement. Other times it's full of dirt or sand. You will need proper technique; strong grip strength; and power in your biceps, back, and legs in order to get through this obstacle.

How to Conquer It

Try not to pull the rope with your upper-body strength but rather by quickly bending at the knees and dropping your body weight, then reeling in the slack. This will save your arm strength and allow you to complete the obstacle faster.

Strength and Power

Another important component of fitness to develop is your strength and power. This is different from the muscular endurance required for navigating obstacles like carries and drags. Pushes and vertical climbs requiring explosive movements—such as flipping a tractor tire or climbing up a vertical wall—will call on your strength and power.

For any of these obstacles, having that strength and power combination is essential for success. If you don't prepare specifically for this type of obstacle, you may find yourself losing minutes at a time and expending valuable energy. Often, these are the obstacles that shock the system and drain you of your reserves. Sometimes, they can even induce cramping if your body is not used to high-power outputs. But never fear: In the following chapters you will learn to prepare accordingly.

Common Obstacles for Strength and Power

Tire Flip

An obstacle requiring an incredible amount of power and brute strength is the tire flip. Participants are expected to flip a large truck tire weighing 150 to 300 pounds end over end anywhere from 4 to 10 times. It requires strength in the quads, hamstrings, biceps, triceps, fingers, lower back, and calves. The power output required for this obstacle can take its toll on running ability later in the race, but it is an opportunity for participants to catch their breath. Therefore, approaching it and completing it correctly are invaluable.

How to Conquer It

Get your fingers under the tire and dead-lift it, keeping your back straight, driving up through your heels, and lifting with your legs. To finish the flip, be sure to step forward and push the tire once you have it vertical.

Wall Climb

An obstacle that incorporates mobility and strength, the wall climb requires you to pull yourself over a single high wall or series of barrier walls. The height of walls can range from 5 to 12 feet (1.5-3.6 m). You'll need upper-body strength and power as well as shoulder and hip mobility to overcome this obstacle.

How to Conquer It

Run at the wall, jump, and grab the top. Brace your feet against the wall, and push off as you pull to get your chest over the wall. Then roll over the top. If necessary, swing a foot over the top of the wall, but beware—if you fall from this position you can severely hurt yourself.

Jump and Leap

You might have seen them in marketing materials promoting obstacle races. Leaps over fire are among the obstacle prototypes of the sport. In addition to leaping over fire, you may need to jump over a series of low barriers, jump from the other side of a high wall, and negotiate similar obstacles. Although these challenges require balance, you'll need leg power and explosiveness in order to get past these obstacles efficiently and safely.

How to Conquer It

Don't fear it. Run hard, leap off one foot, and just keep running!

Rolling Mud Hill or Mud Pit

The rolling mud pits both exhaust you and break your rhythm. Plus you come out of them drenched in mud with heavy shoes and heavier legs. They're essentially a series of steep, slippery, muddy hills with water pits at the bottom.

How to Conquer It

Jump out across the water as far as you can to save time. When climbing, lean forward, dig in your toes, and use your hands to claw your way to the top.

Mental Strength

In many races you'll encounter obstacles designed to challenge you outside the boundaries of just the physical. Some can be trained for, and others not so much. You can expect the following obstacles to test your mental grit and toughness. In addition to these tips, you can learn more about mental training in chapter 14.

Common Obstacles for Mental Strength

Icy Dunk Tank

Tough Mudder can probably be credited for the original icy dunk tank, but it has become a common obstacle in many races. There are variations of the dunk tank, but the principle is similar across races: a large container, sometimes an industrial-size dumpster, filled with ice. It can be placed anywhere along the race route, so you have to be mentally prepared for the shock your warmed-up body will experience as you make your way through an icy tank.

How to Conquer It

Inhale deeply before entering the water, slowly exhaling as you do. Try to stay calm and move fluidly. Once out, resume running as quickly as possible to get your body temperature back up.

Spear Throw

One of the most famous obstacles is the Spartan race spear throw. And while some people consider this obstacle to be a gimmick, others consider it brilliant. You are required to come to a stop, lower your heart rate, control your breathing, and perform an act of skill without error. This is a very difficult thing to do.

How to Conquer It

First, steady your breathing. Next, grab the spear, making sure to hold it at its balance point so that it can rest on your hand without tipping either way. Lift the spear to ear level. The goal is to throw the spear with as few moving parts as possible. Step forward with your left foot, throwing the spear in a flat trajectory or arching slightly upward before descending. You can opt to use your other hand to point at the target as a sight.

Water Crossing

You might encounter several types of water crossings in a race, such as river wading, a lake swim, or an ice bath. Water will be used against you in numerous ways. The most feared and damaging to your race is ice water. The cold temperatures can cause you to lose your breath and mental focus. It can also cause your system to start shutting down. Muscles tighten up, you could cramp, and you might have a difficult time running after a cold dunk.

How to Conquer It

This is similar to the icy dunk tank. Breathe deeply, move deliberately, and stay calm.

Ledge Jump

Ledge jumps are among the greatest tests of mental strength. Jumping off a ledge from a high height can be one of the most intimidating experience of your race.

How to Conquer It

Just commit to the jump. Do not hesitate, and do not think about it. You must know that you will be safe. You must wait until there is a clear spot before you jump so you don't injure someone in the water below. This obstacle is about facing your fears. Mastering them is a key aspect of mental training.

Final Thoughts

Over the course of the next few chapters, we introduce you to exercises and drills that should prove useful in helping you prepare for your upcoming race. It should be everything you need in order to dominate your first event. In addition to building cardiorespiratory and muscular fitness and endurance, you need to acknowledge the value of mental fortitude. Some of the endurance challenges of an obstacle race will require you to dig deep into your heart and soul and find that source of motivation that encouraged you to sign up in the first place. You will need to master the ability to tap into that motivation to conquer the challenges you face and perform at your best. But if you can master the mental side of training and pair it with the physical skills you develop over the next few months, you will undoubtedly have an incredible racing experience.

6

Endurance

Chris noticed he was out of breath into his first race. Never a good runner, now he understands that if he wants to do better in his next race, he'll need to work endurance training into his program. Knowing now that some of the obstacles also test his muscular endurance, he wants to improve his body's ability to lift, carry, and drag heavy objects.

As mentioned in chapter 5, endurance is perhaps the most important of all physical demands required for obstacle racing. Mobility, balance, strength, and power will help you negotiate obstacles, but endurance will get you to the finish line. Applied to obstacle racing, physical endurance is your body's ability to withstand challenges and sustain activity over time.

Endurance consists of both cardiorespiratory and muscular components. Aerobic endurance is the ability of your body to tolerate prolonged activity that challenges your cardiovascular and respiratory systems: your heart and lungs. Walking, jogging, running, swimming, and rowing are all examples of aerobic endurance activities. Muscular endurance is the ability to sustain a long bout or multiple bouts of exertion. Unlike strength and power activities, muscular endurance involves repetitive work carried out over a period of time. Strength and power require your maximal effort, while muscular endurance calls for you to sustain work at submaximal effort.

As part of your training to develop endurance, we provide you with suggestions for running workouts and stand-alone muscular development work. We also encourage you to try sessions in which you integrate aerobic and muscular endurance through circuit training, and we give you examples. Circuit training combines bouts of aerobic activity with running and muscular endurance exercises like push-ups and pull-ups, all of which you will learn more about throughout this chapter. We start with running workouts.

Training to Run

In this program, you'll do a running workout most days of the week. To measure your progress, it's important to get an idea of your pace early on in your training. A quick way to get a basic estimate of your pace is to use the time it took for you to run a mile as part of your fitness program. This can be helpful as a benchmark, but if one of your long-term goals is to be a competitive or serious obstacle runner, you'll want to track your 5K pace as well. You can do this during your first running workout, which, as you'll see in chapter 10, is an easy run of 20 to 30 minutes. You can run on a treadmill or use a sports watch with GPS to track your pace once you've reached a distance of 5K (3.1 miles). You can track improvements in pace on a regular basis using through your running workouts.

As a general rule, during run training you should increase mileage by no more than 10 percent per week. If you are a beginner with minimal running experience, sometimes it's best to focus on recording the time you spend jogging or running rather than total distance. You may need to alternate bouts of walking with jogging (what we call wogging). In this case, increase the total time you spend running by up to 10 percent per week. Record your progress along the way, and make note of how much time you spend jogging and walking. Every time you run, try to spend a little more time running (versus walking) while keeping in mind the weekly 10 percent increase.

Distance Runs

Each week you should do a distance run. A good starting point may be a 30-minute or 3-mile (5K) run. This should be a slow, comfortable run. At first, you'll use it to build endurance, but as you progress through your training program and try other running sessions, your long run will serve as a form of active recovery. It will, believe it or not, loosen up your muscles, clear your mind, and help you mentally prepare for your more rigorous training sessions. During your distance runs, remember to fuel correctly (see more in chapter 4) to simulate race-day preparation and to get your body used to functioning off of the fuel as you continue to run. Your long runs will get progressively longer as you continue to train. Try not to add more than a mile to your long run each week unless you have been training consistently at longer distances. A slow progression is a safe progression, and you can improve only if you continue to stay healthy.

Intervals

An interval session alternates segments of running at a challenging pace with bouts of an easy jog or walk. Intervals improve your anaerobic fitness, which comes in handy for power training and moves like jumping or leaping as well as climbing up steep hills. These running workouts will also help you improve your endurance, which you'll notice on your long runs. Throughout the course of this training program, you will progress through three interval-running workouts.

The first workout employs a work-to-rest ratio of 2:1. So, for example, you'll run hard for 80 seconds, then recover for 40 seconds with an easy jog or walk. You'll repeat the segments of 80-second work: 40-second rest for 5 to 10 sets, depending on where you are in your training program. An interval workout with a 2:1 work-to-rest ratio like this one improves your recovery time and foot speed and boosts your pacing.

The second type of interval session you will do is a half-mile (800 m) run with stretches of an easy jog and walk for a quarter mile (400 m). For these repeats, you'll run at 110 percent of your 5K race pace. For example, if you run a 10-minute mile (9.6 km per hour, or kmh), your interval run would be at 6.6 mph (10.6 kmh). Half-mile repeats will improve your speed, recovery, and lactic acid threshold. Complete anywhere from 4 to 8 repeats, gradually increasing the number of repetitions as you become more fit. The 800-meter repeats are a great distance to use for interval training because you can run fast enough to improve your anaerobic strength while still boosting your aerobic conditioning and speed.

Finally, once you've built up the endurance, you'll do sets of a single-mile run at your 5K race pace followed by bouts of 2-minute recovery or, alternatively, a light jog around the track. You'll do a total of four to six sets of these mile repeats. Mile repeats will boost your lactic threshold and improve your endurance. They are among the best ways to increase your overall running ability and physical and mental toughness.

Hill Repeats

For years, traditional runners have used hill running and repeats to build leg strength and power, increase stride length, and improve endurance. For an obstacle athlete, hill running has a very terrain-specific benefit. Across the course of an obstacle race, you are guaranteed to encounter hills of various types: rolling, ascending, descending, and steep climbs. Hill repeats will not only strengthen your legs and build your fitness but will also help you mentally prepare for a course with varying inclines. The four distinct hill repeats you will complete as part of your training program are sprint, middle distance, long distance, and hike repeats.

Sprint Hill Repeats

For sprint hill repeats, you will pick a hill with an incline from 5 to 25 percent. You can also do this on some treadmills, but we prefer you do this outside when possible because it will better simulate the terrain and conditions you can expect on race day. Sprint up the hill for 10 to 40 seconds. If you are a beginner, you may want to start with 10-second bouts. Your recovery time will vary depending on whether or not your specific running session will focus on endurance or power. A brief recovery time, from 20 to 45 seconds, emphasizes endurance, while a longer recovery time of 1 to 3 minutes will allow your legs enough time to recover in order to give an all-out, explosive effort, thus emphasizing power. You'll do up to 8 sets.

Middle-distance Hill Repeats

Next are middle-distance hill repeats. You'll look for an incline of around 5 to 10 percent, hill or treadmill, and run as fast as you can for 45 to 90 seconds. Recovery should last no longer than a minute. If outdoors, jogging downhill should provide you with ample recovery time. You'll do a total of 6 to 8 sets.

Long Hill Repeats

Long hill repeats can be done on a treadmill. When outdoor hill access is limited due to seasonality or geography, long hill repeats are a great alternative. You'll run 90 seconds to 5 minutes uphill at a mild incline of 3 to 5 percent while maintaining a strong pace. Your pace shouldn't dip much below the pace you currently use for your long run. Recovery will last 1 to 3 minutes with an easy jog or walk, with an adjustment to the incline if needed. You'll do a total of 4 to 6 sets. Long hill repeats will help you build strength, endurance, and lactic threshold.

Hike Repeats

Finally, hike repeats help you get used to the brutal climbing you may face in a mountainous obstacle race. It can be considered a more advanced hill repeat, perhaps best suited for a treadmill that can adjust up to 45 percent. You'll pick a duration, between a 5- and 20-minute climb, and adjust the incline throughout the workout. You can adjust the incline anywhere from 3 to 10 times. Aim for an incline of 20 to 45 percent.

Tempo Runs

The tempo run increases speed, lactic threshold, pacing, and endurance all at once. This type of run is more common among mid- to long-distance runners, but obstacle athletes can benefit from this running session. For the tempo run, you'll cover 3 to 6 miles at 85 to 90 percent of your 10K race pace, so it's faster than your distance runs. Depending on where you are in your training program, you will complete a tempo run about once a week.

Trail Runs

As often as you can, try to get out and run on trails as opposed to a treadmill, track, or road. The idea is to get your lower body, particularly your quads, calves, and ankles, used to running on uneven terrain and the running rigors of an obstacle race. A trail run does not need to be nearly as long as your long-distance run because it tends to wear you out much more quickly. However, it can be useful to do some of your interval training on the trails. One way to simulate a race during a trail run is to cross streams and rivers when you can, or at least dip your shoes in, to get used to running with wet and muddy shoes. You may find that your legs fatigue more quickly with the added weight of the mud and water on your feet.

Integrating distance, intervals, hills, and tempo workouts into your program will help you improve your endurance more than if you were to do only long-distance running. In general, you'll do three to five running workouts each week. Table 6.1 shows a sample four-week running plan so you can get an idea of what your running program will look like within your overall obstacle race training plan. We'll fill in the details for your other training days in part II, which details workouts and specific training plans.

Table 6.1 **Example of a Four-Week Running Plan (Weeks 1-4)**

Sunday	Monday	Tuesday	Wednesday	Thursday	Friday	Saturday
		Sprint hill repeats (4 times)		Intervals: 2:1 ratio (5 sets)		Distance: 3 miles or 30 min
		Middle-distance hill repeats		Tempo run: 15 minutes (plus warm-up)		Distance: 3.25 miles or 33 min
		Long hill repeats: 90 sec work + 3 min recovery (4 sets)		Intervals: 2:1 ratio (6 sets)		Distance: 3.5 miles or 35 min
		Sprint hill repeats (5 times)		Tempo run: 18 minutes (plus warm-up)		Distance: 3.75 miles or 38 min

Cross-Training

Even though running will shape the bulk of your aerobic endurance training, you can use other aerobic activities as a complement and means of cross-training. Incorporating rowing, swimming, biking, and similar activities can help you continue to improve and maintain aerobic endurance during times when your feet may be too sore to run. Some can also help you improve muscular endurance.

Rowing

If you can manage to get your hands on a rowing machine, it can be an incredible asset. Rowing is low impact and a good alternative to running that takes the pounding off of your feet, knees, and ankles and allows you to keep your training at a high intensity. Rowing is a great way to develop cardiovascular strength and aerobic endurance while also improving muscular endurance in your posterior chain (hamstrings, glutes, lower back, and upper back).

To get the most out of rowing, make sure your technique is correct: 60 percent of your power comes from the legs, 20 percent from the core, and 20 percent from the arms. The motion begins from the legs as you drive through your heels. Seamlessly and gently transition your lower back into the pull, and finish by pulling the handle into your abdomen, keeping your back straight. To return to your starting position, release your arms first and then your core, then finally bend at the knees. Reach far forward so that your back bends no more than 45 degrees forward.

For endurance, try rowing intervals of varying distances ranging from 200 to 1,000 meters. A great way to train with rowing intervals is to intersperse strength work such as squats and lunges in between rounds of rowing or to alternate brief periods of running with intervals of rowing.

Swimming

If you have access to a pool or similar aquatic facilities, swimming is another great way to cross-train. Like rowing, swimming is a low-impact activity that can help you build and maintain aerobic endurance. Swimming can help you not only develop aerobic capacity but also build muscular endurance in the shoulders, arms, and lower body. Swimming can also help with hip flexibility and strength, which will come in handy for crawling and climbing obstacles.

Intervals are a basic swimming workout you can use in building endurance. You start by swimming up to 400 meters at an easy pace for a warm-up, then alternate intervals of 100 meters swimming fast with 30 seconds of rest. You can do up to 8 sets of this, then cool down with an easy swim of 200 to 400 meters. (Note that many pools in the United States are 25 yards long, so use the same numbers here in yards.)

Biking

Biking, another low-impact aerobic activity, can also strengthen and improve muscular endurance in the legs and glutes as well as hip flexors and extensors. It also gives the soles of your feet (plantar fascia muscles) a break from the wear and tear of running and jumping. On days when your legs and feet may be too sore to run or after an especially challenging race, you can try biking to maintain your aerobic fitness.

For a biking workout, you can take an easy bike ride in the same capacity as you would an easy run. You can ride outdoors for 45 to 60 minutes, selecting the terrain of your choice. Alternatively, you can try an indoor cycling class or use an indoor cycle on your own.

Muscular Endurance Training

Unlike running, muscular endurance training typically involves repeated completions of a move or sequence of moves designed to improve your muscles' ability to withstand work over time. A great way to put these exercises together as a workout—and one option that is popular because it is efficient and easy to set up—is in a circuit. In circuit training, you'll cycle through a series of exercises in a row, performing them with good form while trying to do as much as you can for a set time period (30-45 seconds) or for a set number of repetitions (10-12).

Rest between exercises will be minimal, just enough to prepare for the following exercise (10-20 seconds, for example); you'll take a longer rest once you've completed the cycle of exercises (in other words, the circuit). You may also include some bouts of running or other cardiorespiratory exercise mixed in a circuit. Circuits are a great way to develop muscular endurance while gaining cardiovascular strength all at once—and it burns a ton of calories while you do it.

In addition to circuits, you can use other effective forms of muscular endurance training to improve your performance.

Tabata Training

Tabata includes 8 rounds of 20 seconds of high-intensity work followed by a 10-second recovery period, for a total of 4 minutes. Tabata training drives your muscles into oxygen debt and then failure, resulting in massive endurance gains and a boost in mitochondrial density.

Burnout Training

This training calls for the completion of one exercise for approximately 5 to 10 repetitions at a light weight, then a rest of 5 seconds. Gradually add more weight (up to 5 pounds) each round until you hit muscle failure, then work your way back down the ladder. The burnout can also be completed by adjusting rep counts on body-weight exercises. (Here is an example: 1 push-up, 5-second recovery, 2 push-ups, 5-second recovery, all the way up to 10 or 15 repetitions.) The burnout will teach your body to function when it has very little oxygen to operate on.

Superset Training

One of the best ways to develop muscular endurance is to complete a superset. The superset requires you to complete 2 to 4 exercises in succession using the same muscle group. An example of a superset is a set of bent-knee deadlifts followed by squats, both of which are exercises we describe in depth later in this chapter. The superset places an extraordinary amount of stress on the muscle, bringing it into oxygen debt and often right to the brink of muscle failure. It can be an uncomfortable way to train but has unquestioned results.

AMRAP

AMRAP stands for as many rounds as possible, and it can be considered a variation of circuit training. With an AMRAP workout, you complete a series of 2 to 5 exercises as many rounds through as you can over a specific time period, which typically ranges from 8 to 20 minutes.

Lower-Body Exercises

No matter how you choose to organize muscular endurance exercises into a workout, it's important to choose exercises that work all the major muscle groups. Let's get into the exercises for muscular endurance applied to obstacle racing. Although the number of sets and reps you complete will vary in this program depending on the workout, to build muscular endurance, you would generally complete 2-3 sets of 12-20 reps of each exercise.

LUNGE

Primary Muscles Worked

Entire leg complex: quadriceps, glutes, hamstrings, calves; progression also works hips, obliques

Start

Stand tall with abdominals engaged, feet about hip-width apart (see figure *a*).

Move

1. Take a big step forward with the right leg.
2. Drop your glutes and hips toward the floor so that your right quad and left lower leg

a

(continued)

LUNGE *(continued)*

are parallel to the floor (see figure *b*). Your leg should bend to 90 degrees, but your knee should not pass your toe. Your back knee should come within 1 inch (2.5 cm) of the floor.

3. Keep your back straight with your chest out and shoulders back, and use your core strength to keep your shoulders from pulling forward.

4. To return to your starting position, engage your quad and drive off of your front foot.

5. Alternate legs and complete with your left leg (see figure *c*).

b

Variation: Turning Lunge

To engage the obliques and hips as well as work on agility, try the turning lunge variation.

Start

Stand tall with abdominals engaged, feet about hip-width apart.

Move

c

1. Raise your right leg while simultaneously pivoting your left foot so your body turns to the right as you get into a lunge position.

2. Return to start, pushing off the right heel.

3. Alternate legs and complete with your left leg.

Safety Tip

Keep your abdominals engaged and back strong during this exercise.

Training Tips

\ Work up to lunging in reps of 30 to 200 and sprinting immediately upon completion.

\ Also try adding lunges as a recovery exercise between running intervals.

SQUAT

Primary Muscles Worked

Hip flexors, quadriceps, glutes, hamstrings

Start

Stand tall with abdominals engaged and feet hip-width apart (see figure *a*). Maintain proper posture with your chest out and shoulders back.

Move

1. Push your hips back and lower your glutes toward the floor (see figure *b*).

2. Keep your back straight and heels on the floor as you lower into a squat.

3. To stand, drive through your heels, exhaling on the effort.

Safety Tip

Keep your abdominals engaged and back strong during this exercise.

Training Tips

↘ To add a challenge to the body-weight squat, you have a couple choices. First, you can add weight with dumbbells in a shoulder carry or hang (see figures *c* and *d*).

↘ You can also adjust the surface to an unsteady one with the use of a BOSU or balance pad (see figure *e*).

a

b

c

d

e

BENT-KNEE DEADLIFT

Primary Muscles Worked

Hip flexors, quadriceps, glutes, hamstrings

Equipment Needed

Dumbbells or barbell

Start

a

1. Stand tall with abdominals engaged and feet hip-width apart.
2. Maintain proper posture with your chest out and shoulders back.
3. Dumbbells should be in a hang-carry hold (see figure *a*).
4. If using a barbell, hold with an overhand grip wider than hip-width apart.

Move

b

1. Press your hips back as you lower your glutes toward the floor. Try to lower so that your thighs are parallel to the floor.
2. As you lower your glutes, lower the dumbbells or barbell as well. Keep your back straight and heels on the floor throughout the move (see figure *b*).
3. Squeeze your glutes tight through the entire movement and keep your spine pulled in toward your navel.
4. Hold for a moment.
5. To return to your starting position, press your hips forward, driving through your heels and continuing to squeeze your glutes.
6. Stand tall at the top.

Safety Tip

Keep your abdominals engaged, shoulders back, and back strong during this exercise.

Training Tip

The bent-knee deadlift is also a great preparatory exercise for some of the total-body power exercises you will learn later in this section.

STRAIGHT-LEG DEADLIFT

Primary Muscles Worked

Glutes, hamstrings, back

Equipment Needed

Dumbbells or barbells

Start

1. Stand tall with abdominals engaged and feet about hip-width apart.
2. Hold dumbbells or barbell in front of you (see figure a).
3. If using a barbell, hold with an overhand grip wider than hip-width apart.
4. Again, focus on keeping your chest out and shoulders back and squeezing your glutes tight.

a

Move

1. Drive your hips back and lower the weights as close to your legs as possible (see figure b).
2. Keep your back strong and straight by engaging your abdominal muscles as you lower your torso forward until the weights are at shin level.
3. Drive your hips forward, squeezing your glutes and pressing through your heels.
4. You should feel tension in the hamstrings throughout this exercise.

b

Safety Tip

Keep your abdominals engaged and back straight during this exercise.

Leg Strength Exercises for Recovery

When running obstacle races, people find that it's not their lungs that fail them during the event. Usually it's the muscles in the legs that fatigue first. So training your legs to be impervious to fatigue is essential for success. One of the ways you can do so is to intersperse leg strength exercises between intervals of running.

In an obstacle race you will have spurts of running and cardiorespiratory effort broken up by obstacles requiring strength or power. So when training, a great way to simulate it is to add leg strength to your running workouts. Throwing in squats, lunges, burpees, or broad jumps in between your running intervals is a great way to bring your breathing back under control while still pushing your legs and conditioning them to respond in the face of fatigue. It also teaches your legs to use running as a recovery to loosen up and keep moving when severely fatigued. Try sets of 10 to 100 of any of the previously mentioned exercises as your recovery instead of walking or jogging between running intervals. It will dramatically change how the workout affects your body, and you will make significant gains in muscular endurance in your legs.

Upper-Body and Abdominal Exercises

Your upper-body and abdominal muscles are called on for several obstacles, including walls, rope climbs, crawls, and sustained carries of any kind. The ability to lift and move your own body weight is a must. The exercises in this section improve muscular endurance in your upper body and abdominals.

PUSH-UP

Primary Muscles Worked

Shoulders, triceps, chest, back, abdominals, obliques

Equipment Needed

Mat (optional)

Start

Begin from a straight-arm plank position (hands loaded beneath the shoulders, feet together out behind, and legs straight), with abdominal muscles engaged, pelvis tucked in, and glutes tight (see figure *a*).

a

Move

1. Bend the elbows to lower your body toward the floor with control.

b

2. Lower your body as close to the floor as you can without actually touching it (see figure *b*).

3. Continue to squeeze your abs and glutes, but also squeeze your shoulder blades together at the bottom.

4. Drive through your hands, engaging your chest and triceps to return to your starting position.

Variation: Rotational Push-Up

Once you've mastered the traditional push-up, add a shoulder rotation to further engage the core and work the chest and shoulder muscles.

Start

Get into a straight-arm plank with your abdominal muscles engaged and pelvis tucked under (see figure c).

c

Move

1. Complete the traditional push-up.
2. As you return to your starting position, raise one hand off of the floor and rotate your body, turning your torso until it is perpendicular with the floor.
3. Look up at your hand reaching toward the ceiling (see figure d).
4. Momentarily, only your hand and feet will be on the floor as you will be balancing and supporting your weight using your arm and core muscles.
5. Alternate each time.
6. You can make the rotational push-up simpler by completing the side plank rotation from the forearm instead of planting the hand.

d

Variation: Beginner Push-Up

There are a few ways to modify the push-up for beginners. Most commonly, push-ups can be made easier by simply spreading the feet or completing it from the knees (see figure e). Another modified exercise is to elevate the hands so that they rest on a bench or two parallel chairs and adjust the height of your hands until you have built strength to do push-ups directly on the floor (see figure f).

e

f

Safety Tips

> Keep your abdominals engaged and back strong during this exercise.

> Keep the wrists and hands right below the shoulders throughout this exercise to avoid any strain in the wrists and rotator cuff muscles.

(continued)

PUSH-UP *(continued)*

Training Tips

❱ The push-up doubles as an upper-body strength and shoulder mobility exercise.

❱ Intermediate to advanced athletes can complete a set of push-ups to prepare the arms and core for a strength day, while beginners may do the basic push-up for muscular endurance. You'll see push-ups a lot in your obstacle race training!

BODY-WEIGHT ROW

Primary Muscles Worked

Upper back, shoulders, biceps, grip strength, abdominals

Equipment Needed

Sturdy weighted bar at about hip height or a suspension strap

Start

a

1. Place your body underneath the bar, or grip the straps with tension in the line.
2. Hold on to the grip with both hands about shoulder-width apart with an overhand (neutral) grip.
3. Balance your weight on your heels, is supported by your arms and legs.
4. Keep your feet, hips, and shoulders in alignment.
5. Don't let your hips sag or arch your back.
6. Squeeze the shoulder blades together (retract your shoulders) and engage your abdominals (see figure *a*).

b

Move

1. While keeping your shoulders retracted and abdominals engaged, drive your elbows back and pull your body toward the bar or straps (see figure *b*).
2. Hold for a moment.
3. Return to starting position, controlling your descent.

Safety Tips

❱ To power this exercise, be sure your shoulders are retracted and abdominals are engaged.

❱ Try not to strain your neck or shrug your shoulders excessively because fatigue may set in toward the end of a set.

DUMBBELL ROW

Primary Muscles Worked

Upper back, biceps, lower back, and grip strength

Equipment Needed

Dumbbells

Start

1. Stand tall with abdominals engaged in a staggered or bent-knee stance.
2. Hold dumbbells in your hands, palms facing in (neutral grip).
3. Lean forward with your chest out and shoulders back (see figure *a*).
4. Sit back on your heels to keep the pressure off your lower back.

Move

Drive the elbows back, squeezing the shoulder blades. Maintain your posture (see figure *b*).

Variation: Reverse-Grip Dumbbell Row

↘ For an added challenge to your back and balance, try rows with both palms facing upward.

↘ The row is essentially the same, but your biceps and back are engaged more intensely, and wrist strength is also enhanced.

Safety Tip

If you have any back problems, emphasize placing pressure in your heels.

Training Tips

↘ You can vary the grip in order to mix it up and target your back at various angles. For example, an overhand grip with your palms facing you will target the upper back (see figure *c*).

↘ A rotation within the row from overhand to underhand is a powerful tool in developing your back and biceps strength.

a

b

c

SHOULDER PRESS

Primary Muscles Worked
Shoulders

Equipment Needed
Dumbbells

Start

1. Stand tall with abdominals engaged and feet about hip-width apart or staggered if you need to take pressure off your lower back.

2. Hold a pair of dumbbells so that your elbows are bent and pointing outward at a 90-degree angle at shoulder height (see figure *a*).

Move

a

1. Using your shoulders, drive the weights up overhead until your arms are straight (see figure *b*).

2. Hold for a moment.

3. Return to start slowly.

Training Tips

❯ Don't shrug your shoulders during this exercise or strain your neck. Use your arms.

❯ Opt for a neutral grip (palms turned inward) if you would like to take the pressure off your shoulder joint (see figures *c* and *d*).

b

c

d

PULL-UP

Primary Muscles Worked

Upper and middle back, shoulders, arms, and abdominals

Equipment Needed

Pull-up bar and chair (for modification)

Start

1. Hold on to a pull-up bar so that your hands are about shoulder-width apart with an overhand grip (see figure *a*).
2. Squeeze your shoulder blades together (retract the shoulders) and keep your abdominals engaged.

Move

1. While keeping your shoulders retracted and abdominals engaged, use your arms to pull yourself up toward the bar.
2. Pull yourself up so that your collar bone reaches the bar (see figure *b*).
3. Control your speed as you descend to the starting position.

Variation: Pull-Up Assist With a Chair

An assisted pull-up using a chair is a good way to work up to a pull-up if you don't yet have the upper-body strength. Once you can do a set of 10 to 12 assisted pull-ups, progress to unassisted pull-ups.

Start

1. Hold on to a pull-up bar so that your hands are wider than shoulder-width apart with an overhand grip.
2. Place your feet on a sturdy chair as you hold on to the pull-up bar (see figure *c*).
3. Squeeze your shoulder blades together (retract the shoulders) and keep your abdominals engaged.

a

b

c

(continued)

PULL-UP *(continued)*

Move

1. While keeping your shoulders retracted and abdominals engaged, use your arms to pull yourself up toward the bar.

2. Pull yourself up so that your collar bone reaches the bar (see figure *d*).

3. Use the chair as minimally as possible to help pull yourself up to the bar.

4. Return to start.

Variation: Muscle-Up

If you've mastered the pull-up and can complete a few sets of 10 to 15 reps, you may be ready to progress to muscle-ups. Muscle-ups are an advanced exercise and will prepare you for walls that soar significantly higher than your height.

d

Start

1. Hold on to a pull-up bar so that your hands are about shoulder-width apart with an overhand grip.

2. Squeeze your shoulder blades together (retract the shoulders) and keep your abdominals engaged.

Move

1. While keeping your shoulders retracted and abdominals engaged, use your arms to pull yourself up toward the bar.

e

2. Pull yourself up so that your collar bone reaches the bar.

3. Continue to pull your chest and torso up until your chest is over the bar (see figures *e*).

4. Drive through your hands, using your triceps to press yourself above the bar. The bar should reach hip height (see figure *f*). Ideally, moves 1 and 2 should be one fluid motion.

5. Return to start.

Safety Tips

❭ To power this exercise, be sure your shoulders are retracted and abdominals are engaged.

❭ Try not to strain your neck or shrug your shoulders excessively as you work toward the pull-up or fatigue toward the end of a set.

f

﹨ Form is especially critical with the muscle-ups because you want ensure your arms, upper back, and abs are powering you through the exercise, not your neck and surrounding muscles.

Training Tips

﹨ Vary the grip in order to mix it up and target your upper body at various angles. A narrow underhand grip (for a chin-up) will engage your biceps and, for some, may serve as an alternative regression to build up to an overhand pull-up.

﹨ If you have a pull-up bar with various handle placements, a grip with your hands facing each other is another regression that might help you build up to an overhand pull-up (see figures *g* and *h*).

﹨ We prefer the overhand pull-up because it more closely simulates the challenge of having to haul yourself over a tall wall, but you can try different hand grips in efforts to progress to the traditional pull-up.

g

h

AB ROLLOUT

Primary Muscles Worked

Entire torso: abdominals and obliques

Equipment Needed

Mat or towel (optional) and stability ball or ab rollout device

Start

1. Kneel on a towel or mat with a stability ball or ab rollout device in front of you.
2. Place your hands or elbows on the stability ball or ab rollout device (see figure *a*).

a

Move

1. Squeeze your abs and glutes as you roll the stability ball or ab rollout device forward (see figure *b*).
2. Work up to rolling forward until your arms are overhead and your torso is parallel to the floor.
3. Return to start.

b

Variation: Diagonal Rollout

To emphasize the obliques, try a diagonal rollout. Rather than rolling forward, roll diagonally in front of you (see figure *c*).

Variation: Straight-Leg Rollout

Once you've mastered the basic ab rollout, try it with your legs straight. This progression is much more challenging than the basic ab rollout, so be sure you have mastered form before progressing.

c

Start

Get into a straight-arm plank so that your hands are on either side of the stability ball or rollout device. You should be in the up position of a push-up (see figure *d*).

Move

1. Squeeze your abs and glutes as you roll your arms forward.
2. Work up to rolling forward until your arms are overhead.

Training Tip

You can also do this using an ab wheel or barbells.

d

LEG RAISE

Primary Muscles Worked

Back, abdominals, obliques, and hip flexors

Equipment Needed

Mat or towel (optional)

Start

1. Lie with your back on a mat with your legs extended, heels a few inches above the mat or floor (see figure *a*).
2. Engage your abdominals and tuck your pelvis forward so that your back is flat on the mat.
3. Your arms should be by your sides.

a

Move

1. Using your abdominals, lift your legs until your legs and hips form a 90-degree angle (see figure *b*).
2. Return to start.

b

Safety Tips

- Make sure your back is flat on the mat throughout the duration of this exercise.
- If you feel any rounding in your back so that it loses contact with the mat, shorten the range of motion to this exercise so that you lift up until the point before your back loses contact with the mat.

HIGH-TO-LOW PLANK

Primary Muscles Worked

Core, abdominals, obliques, and arms

Equipment Needed

Mat or towel (optional)

Start

1. Get into a straight-arm plank so that you are in the up part of a push-up (see figure *a*).
2. Squeeze the abdominals and tuck your pelvis under.

Move

1. Bend your left elbow (see figure *b*) and then your right elbow to get into a bent-elbow plank.
2. Hold for a moment.
3. Return to start.
4. Repeat, leading with your right elbow to complete one rep.

a

b

Variation: High-to-Low Plank on Knees

If the straight-leg high-to-low plank is too challenging for you at the start of your training program, try this modification.

Start

1. Get into a modified plank so that your knees are on the mat, back is straight, and arms are straight with your hands on the mat. You should be in the up part of a push-up.
2. Squeeze the abdominals and tuck your pelvis under.

Move

1. Bend your left elbow and then your right elbow to get into a bent-elbow plank.
2. Hold for a moment.
3. Return to start.
4. Repeat, leading with your right elbow to complete one rep.

Training Tip

Make sure your back is flat and core is engaged throughout this exercise.

MOUNTAIN CLIMBER

Primary Muscles Worked
Core, abdominals, obliques, and arms

Equipment Needed
Mat or towel (optional)

Start
1. Get into a straight-arm plank so that you are in the up part of a push-up.
2. Squeeze the abdominals and tuck your pelvis under.

a

Move
1. While in a straight-arm plank, lift your right foot off the floor and tuck your right knee in toward your chest (see figure *a*).
2. As you return to start, lift your left foot off the floor and tuck your left knee in toward your chest (see figure *b*). This completes one rep.

b

Variation: Crossover Mountain Climber
To work on hip flexibility as well, try the crossover mountain climber.

Start
1. Get into a straight-arm plank so that you are in the up part of a push-up.
2. Squeeze the abdominals and tuck your pelvis under.

Move
1. While in a straight-arm plank, lift your right foot off the floor and tuck your right knee in toward your left shoulder.
2. As you return to start, lift your left foot off the floor and tuck your left knee in toward your right shoulder. This completes one rep.

Variation: Push-Up With Mountain Climber
You'll see this progression often in your training program. The push-up with mountain climber engages the upper body as well as the core, abdominals, obliques, and hips.

Start
1. Get into a straight-arm plank so that you are in the up part of a push-up.
2. Squeeze the abdominals and tuck your pelvis under.

(continued)

MOUNTAIN CLIMBER (continued)

Move

1. Do a push-up and return to a straight-arm plank.
2. While in a straight-arm plank, lift your right foot off the floor and tuck your right knee in toward your chest.
3. As you return to start, lift your left foot off the floor and tuck your left knee in toward your chest. The push-up and alternating mountain climber complete one rep.

Safety Tip

Keep your back flat and abdominals engaged throughout this exercise.

HANGING KNEE RAISE

Primary Muscles Worked

Core, abdominals, shoulders, forearms, hip flexors, and hip extensors

Equipment Needed

Pull-up bar

a

Start

1. Hold on to a pull-up bar so that your hands are wider than shoulder-width apart with an overhand grip (see figure *a*).
2. Squeeze your shoulder blades together (retract the shoulders) and keep your abdominals engaged.

Move

1. Using your abdominals and keeping your back strong, bend your knees and raise them toward your chest (see figure *b*).
2. Return to start in a controlled motion.

Variation: Alternating Knee Raise

Start

1. Hold on to a pull-up bar so that your hands are wider than shoulder-width apart with an overhand grip.
2. Squeeze your shoulder blades together (retract the shoulders) and keep your abdominals engaged.

b

Move

1. Using your abdominals and keeping your back strong, bend your right knee and raise it toward your chest (see figure *c*).

2. Return to start in a controlled motion.

3. Repeat with the left leg to complete one rep.

Variation: Ankles to Bar

Start

1. Hold on to a pull-up bar so that your hands are wider than shoulder-width apart with an overhand grip.

2. Squeeze your shoulder blades together (retract the shoulders) and keep your abdominals engaged.

c

Move

1. Using your abdominals and keeping your back strong, bend your knees and raise them toward your chest.

2. As you raise your knees, lean back with your knees tucked in, then extend your legs so that your ankles touch the pull-up bar (see figure *d*).

3. Return to start in a controlled motion.

Safety Tips

Keep your abdominals engaged during this exercise. If you have a weak back or any back problems, avoid this exercise and modifications.

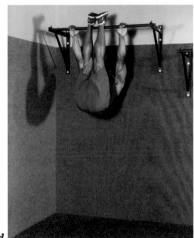

d

Total-Body Exercises

Obstacle racing challenges your body as an integrated unit, so it's important to include total-body exercises in your muscular endurance program. The following total-body moves will also help prepare you for strength and power training.

SQUAT WITH SHOULDER PRESS

Primary Muscles Worked

Quadriceps, hamstrings, glutes, shoulders, and arms

Equipment Needed

Dumbbells, barbell, or kettlebells

Start

1. Stand tall with abdominals engaged and back straight.
2. Hold a pair of dumbbells, kettlebells, or a barbell in a shoulder-carry position (see figure *a*).

Move

1. Push your hips back and complete a squat (see figure *b*).
2. Push through your heels to return to a standing position while simultaneously pressing the weight overhead (see figure *c*).
3. Remember, just as with all strength exercises, exhale on the effort.

a

b

c

LUNGE WITH CURL AND PRESS

Primary Muscles Worked
Quadriceps, hamstrings, glutes, calves, shoulders, and arms

Equipment Needed
Dumbbells

Start

1. Stand tall with abdominals engaged and back straight.
2. Keep your chest out and shoulders back.
3. Hold a pair of dumbbells in a hang-carry position at your sides (see figure *a*).

a

Move

1. Step the right foot forward to bring your right thigh parallel to the floor in a lunge position; at the same time, perform a biceps curl with the dumbbells, bending at the elbow until the heads of the dumbbells are near shoulder height (see figure *b*).
2. From the lunge, press the dumbbells overhead to complete a shoulder press (see figure *c*) as you return to start position, pushing off the heel of the front leg.
3. Return the weights to your side in a controlled manner and repeat with the left leg.

b

Training Tip
Use a weight lighter than what you used for the squat with shoulder press (thruster).

c

KETTLEBELL SWING

Primary Muscles Worked

Quadriceps, hamstrings, glutes, hips, core, arms

Equipment Needed

Kettlebell

Start

1. The best way to describe the kettlebell swing is a controlled, explosive movement.
2. Stand tall with abdominals engaged and back straight, feet about a shoulder-width apart.
3. Keep the chest out and shoulders back.
4. Bend the knees and pick the weight up off the floor (see figure *a*).
5. Allow it to swing between your legs (see figure *b*).

a

Move

1. Drive the hips forward, squeezing the glutes. This motion will drive the weight up to eye level, where it will reach its apex (see figure *c*).
2. Don't use arm strength to move the weight. It should point in approximately the same direction your arms.
3. Allow the weight to descend between your legs as your hips push back. Your shoulders will rock forward.
4. Do your best to use your core strength to keep your shoulders from pulling forward too aggressively. Repeat.

b

Safety Tips

- Keep your back straight and strong throughout this exercise.
- This is an advanced move, so be sure your back and core muscles are strong enough to power this exercise.
- Power comes from the glutes.

c

BURPEE

Primary Muscles Worked

Quadriceps, hamstrings, chest, shoulders, abdominals, and obliques

Start

From a standing position, squat, keeping your back strong and abdominals engaged (see figure a).

Move

a

1. Jump your legs back behind you to get into a straight-arm plank position (see figure b). To return to start, push your body up, use your abs to tuck your knees in to get back into a low squat (see figure c), and jump up (see figure d).

2. Land softly as you lower into a squat for the next repetition.

Variation: With Tuck Jump

b

To add a challenge to your lower body and work on power, when you tuck in your legs from a low squat position, jump upward and tuck your knees into your chest, then land gently.

Safety Tip

Keep your back strong and your core engaged, and try to keep your back from rounding throughout the exercise.

c

Training Tip

The burpee is a total-body exercise that works your strength, power, and agility as well as cardiorespiratory and muscular endurance. Learn to love the burpee; you'll see it a lot throughout your training!

d

Final Thoughts

Completing an obstacle race depends on endurance. Building up endurance takes time and patience, and we'll guide you there with a sound plan complete with running and muscular development exercises. As an obstacle athlete, you'll need to balance endurance training with strength and power. In chapter 7, we go over mobility and balance, two critical components that will help you hold your body together as you balance endurance and strength as well as prepare you for race-specific obstacles.

7

Mobility and Balance

Chris expected balancing over logs and crawling over low barriers to be some of the easier obstacles in the race, giving him a chance to catch his breath. Although his balance is pretty good, he found it difficult to get under barriers. Chris wants to increase his mobility and maintain his balance while working on all the other aspects of fitness he needs to in order to crush his next race.

By now, you might have noticed that obstacle race training calls for a multifaceted approach. Although we have outlined four specific types of physical requirements necessary for obstacle racing, some of the requirements often overlap. That's especially the case with mobility and balance. Applied to obstacle racing, mobility and balance cover dynamic flexibility, coordination, core stability and strength, and proper landing mechanics. Working on your mobility and balance will also help with long-term injury prevention. It should go without saying, but it's important to remember that even though mobility and balance are often the most overlooked components in training programs, they are two of the most critical to complement and optimize your training results. This chapter covers exercises and provides you with guidelines on when to work on mobility and balance.

When to Train Mobility and Balance

You can work on mobility and balance during the warm-up, cooldown, and actual work bout of your training sessions. As with most components of obstacle racing, you'll need to warm up before working on them. Walking, wogging (a combination of walking and jogging), jogging, or other aerobic activity for at least 5 minutes will elevate your body's core temperature and prepare you for activity. Once your body is warm, you can engage in a specific warm-up that will prepare you for your workout.

In most cases, your specific warm-up will integrate mobility and balance with dynamic flexibility, core, and even basic strength exercises. The actual workout may also contain mobility and balance exercises, particularly if you are completing a scaled-back active recovery session. In an active recovery session, you'll focus on flexibility as well as light balance and core exercise in order to give your body a break from your more rigorous training workouts while maintaining mobility. However, even on days focused on strength, you can work on mobility by ensuring that you move through the full range of motion (ROM) for all exercises. The cool-down part of your workout will give you a chance to work on mobility and balance with static stretches and other flexibility exercises.

Dynamic Flexibility and Mobility Exercise

The following exercises will help you with obstacles that require any leg swinging or hooking as well as external hip rotation, such as walls, marine hurdles, and very low crawls. The last five exercises also engage the shoulders in order to help you with obstacles that involve swinging and mobility across the shoulder muscles such as monkey bars, very low crawls, and reaches. As a bonus, these dynamic flexibility exercises can prepare your body for strength and running sessions. Although the number of sets and reps will vary depending on the workout you're completing, in general, you'll do at least one set of 6-12 reps of each of the following exercises.

FORWARD LEG SWING

Primary Muscles Worked

Hip flexors, quadriceps, and hamstrings

Start

Stand tall close to a wall or other base to support your balance (see figure *a*).

Move

1. Lift your right leg in front of you and swing it forward and backward (see figures *b* and *c*) with control for a total of 8 reps.

2. Switch and repeat with left leg.

a

Safety Tips

\ Use momentum to swing your legs, but be sure you are in control of the movement by keeping your abdominal muscles engaged and back strong.

\ Focus on moving through the full range of motion as allowed by your flexibility.

Variation

As a progression, do a calf raise with the leg that's planted on the floor as you lift the swinging leg forward. This will prepare your calves for any activity involving the lower body, such as running or jumping.

b

c

SIDE-TO-SIDE LEG SWING

Primary Muscles Worked

Hip flexors, quadriceps, hamstrings, adductors, and abductors

Start

1. Stand tall facing a wall about an arm's-length away (see figure *a*).
2. Place hands against the wall for balance.

Move

1. Lift your right leg outward and swing outward and back inward (see figures *b* and *c*) with control for a total of 8 reps.
2. Switch and repeat with left leg.

Safety Tips

❯ Use momentum to swing your legs, but be sure you are in control of the movement by keeping your abdominal muscles engaged and back strong.

❯ Focus on moving through the full range of motion as allowed by your flexibility.

Variation

As a progression, do a calf raise with the leg that's planted on the floor as you lift the swinging leg outward. This will help prepare your calves for any activity involving the lower body, such as running or jumping.

a

b

c

STANDING KNEE-UP

Primary Muscles Worked

Hip flexors, quadriceps, adductors, and abductors

Start

Stand tall with the abdominal muscles engaged and pelvis tucked under (see figure *a*).

Move

1. Bend and raise your right knee above waist level (see figure *b*) and rotate or extend outward (see figure *c*) and back in.

2. Lower right leg to start.

3. Alternate legs and do a total of 12 reps (6 each leg).

a

b

c

STANDING LEG-OVER

Primary Muscles Worked

Adductors, abductors, hip flexors, quadriceps, and hamstrings

Equipment Needed

Bar stool or chair that's midthigh to waist height, depending on your flexibility

Start

1. Stand tall with abdominals and glutes engaged.
2. Stand a few inches away from a bar stool or other stable, chair-height item (see figure *a*).

Move

1. Using your abs and squeezing your quads, lift your right leg and sweep it over the height of the stable item (see figure *b*).
2. Tap the floor on the other side, then sweep the right leg back to start (see figure *c*).
3. Do recommended number of reps.

Safety Tips

⟍ During the sweep, keep your leg straight but knee slightly bent so that it's not locked.

⟍ Use your core and legs to power this exercise.

Variation

To emphasize the hip flexor and extend the stretch through the hip adductors and abductors, bend at the knee as you raise your leg. You may need to adjust the height of the barrier so that it's lower than the height used for the straight-leg leg-over.

a

b

c

SIDE LUNGE

Primary Muscles Worked

Adductors, abductors, quadriceps, hip flexors, hamstrings, and obliques

Start

Stand tall with abdominals engaged and feet about hip-width apart. Option: Hold a dumbbell or kettlebell for added weight (see figure *a*).

Move

1. Raise your right leg, take a big step to your right, and lower the glutes so that you are in a side lunge (see figure *b*).
2. Keep both heels on the floor with toes pointing forward.
3. Return to start and alternate legs to complete a rep.

Variation: Cossack Squat

Try the cossack squat for a deeper stretch in the hips and if you have no history of knee injuries or joint pain.

a

b

Start

Stand with your abdominals engaged and feet approximately 2 to 2.5 times wider than hip-width apart.

Move

1. Drop your hips and glutes toward your right leg into a deep lunge, resting most of your weight on your right heel.
2. Move back slowly to start, pushing off the right heel, and switch to the left leg to complete a rep.

Safety Tip

The side lunge is often an exercise in which many discover limitations in hip flexibility. Start slowly with the exercise, moving through your body's range of motion. Over time and with practice, you will improve range of motion through the hips, abductors, and adductors.

Training Tip

Master the side lunge before moving onto the cossack squat.

GROINER

Primary Muscles Worked

Hip flexors, hamstrings, and adductors

Start

Get into a straight-arm plank (the up part of a push-up) with your abdominal muscles engaged and pelvis tucked under (see figure *a*).

Move

1. Drive your right knee toward your right arm (see figure *b*) and place the heel of your right foot outside of your right hand (see figure *c*).
2. Hold momentarily to feel a stretch in the quadriceps and hip flexors in your left leg.
3. Return to start and alternate legs to complete a rep.

Variation: Groiner With T Stabilization

1. While in the groiner position with your right heel next to your right hand, extend the opposite (left) arm and rotate your torso so that your left fingertips are pointing toward the ceiling. This will extend the stretch to work your anterior shoulder and pectoral muscles.
2. Alternate sides to complete one rep.

Safety Tips

\ Keep your abdominals engaged and back strong during this exercise.

\ Try the progression once you have mastered the basic groiner and have developed flexibility along the shoulders and chest.

\ Avoid the progression at the start of your exercise program if you have any recent shoulder injuries or similar condition.

a

b

c

REVERSE LUNGE WITH TWIST

Primary Muscles Worked

Entire leg complex: quadriceps, glutes, hamstrings, calves; obliques, and shoulders

Equipment Needed

Dumbbell or kettlebell

Start

1. Stand tall with abdominals engaged and feet about hip-width apart (see figure *a*).
2. Hold a dumbbell or kettlebell for added weight.

Move

1. Take a big step backward with the right leg (see figure *b*).
2. Twist toward your left side and extend back until you feel a stretch in the right obliques, hip flexors, and quadriceps (see figure *c*).
3. Return to start, pushing off the left heel.
4. Alternate legs and repeat on the other side.

Safety Tip

Keep your abdominals engaged and back strong during this exercise.

a

b

c

SUMO SQUAT

Primary Muscles Worked

Quadriceps, glutes, hamstrings, adductors, and abductors

Start

Stand tall with abdominals engaged, feet wider than shoulder-width apart, and toes and knees pointing outward slightly. Option: Hold a dumbbell or kettlebell for added weight (see figure a).

a

Move

1. Lower your glutes toward the floor until your upper thighs are parallel to the floor (see figure b).

2. Keep your knees pointing outward in the same direction as your toes.

Safety Tip

If you have any knee problems, avoid this exercise.

b

OVERHEAD SQUAT

Primary Muscles Worked

Hip flexors, quadriceps, glutes, hamstrings, shoulders, and back

Start

1. Stand tall with abdominals engaged and feet hip-width apart.

2. Raise your arms overhead so that they are next to your ears (see figure a).

Move

1. Bend at the hips and lower your glutes toward the floor.

a

(continued)

OVERHEAD SQUAT *(continued)*

2. Keep your back straight and heels on the floor as you lower into a squat (see figure *b*).
3. Try to keep your arms from floating forward.
4. Return to start.

Variation: Squat With Anterior Arm Raise

If your upper back and lats are too tight to hold arms overhead, try this modification.

Start

Stand tall with abdominals engaged, feet hip-width apart, and arms by your side.

a

Move

1. As you get into a squat, raise your arms forward until they are at shoulder height.
2. Return to start.

Safety Tip

Keep your abdominals engaged and back strong during this exercise.

HAND WALK

Primary Muscles Worked

Hamstrings, shoulders, back, and abdominals

Start

Stand tall with abdominals engaged and feet hip-width apart.

Move

1. Reach toward the floor slowly while keeping your legs straight (see figure *a*).
2. Walk your hands forward (see figure *b*) until you are in a straight-arm plank (the up part of a push-up) (see figure *c*).
3. Make sure your abdominal muscles are engaged and back is straight.
4. To return to start, walk your hands back toward your toes and roll up slowly to return to a stand.

a

b

Safety Tips

❧ Keep your abdominals engaged and back strong during this exercise as well as your legs straight throughout.

❧ If you have limited flexibility in your hamstrings, bend your knees slightly during the walk-out into a straight-arm plank and walk back to your toes.

c

SPIDERMAN CLIMBER

Primary Muscles Worked

Hamstrings, shoulders, back, abdominals, obliques, and hips

Start

Get into a low plank position, with forearms on the ground, elbows directly beneath your shoulders, and toes planted (see figure *a*).

Move

a

1. Lift your right leg, bend at the knee, and rotate the hip outward as you reach your right knee in toward your right elbow (see figure *b*).

2. Return to start and repeat with the left leg.

3. Continue for the recommended number of reps. Your obliques and hips will fire as you develop range of motion in your hips and improve strength relevant to any low crawl obstacle you encounter.

Variation: With Hand Walk

b

You can combine this exercise with hand walks to stretch out and warm up the hamstrings and hip flexors in one exercise. Simply do a hand walk until you are in a straight-arm plank position and tuck in the right knee toward your right elbow and repeat on the other leg before returning to a stand. Do the recommended number of reps.

Safety Tip

Keep your abdominals engaged, back strong, and pelvis tucked under during this exercise.

Balance and Core Exercises

The following balance and core exercises will help you develop obstacle-specific balance and core stability for crawling through tunnels or low barriers (barbed wire, netted rope, wood planks) and walking over narrow beams as well as slippery and other unsteady surfaces.

SINGLE-LEG BALANCE WITH REACH

Primary Muscles Worked

Hamstrings, glutes, calves, and back

Start

Stand tall with abdominals engaged and feet hip-width apart (see figure *a*).

a

Move

1. Balance on your right leg as you lean and reach forward (slightly out and down) with both arms (see figure *b*).
2. Simultaneously lift and extend your left leg behind you.
3. Hold and balance for a moment.
4. Return to start and repeat on opposite side.

Variation: Single-Leg Deadlift

For the move segment, reach toward your toes. This will further challenge your balance and stretch out the hamstrings.

b

Training Tip

Keep your abdominals engaged and back strong during this exercise (for both the reach and progression deadlift).

Other Tip

The single-leg balance with reach and single-leg deadlift are both good warm-up and body preparation exercises for lunges and other leg work.

SINGLE-LEG SQUAT

Primary Muscles Worked

Hamstrings, glutes, quads, and calves

Start

1. Stand tall with abdominals engaged and feet hip-width apart. This exercise can be performed as a bodyweight exercise or with the use of dumbbells or a suspension device.

2. Balance so that you are standing on your right leg (see figure *a*).

a

Move

1. Bend the right knee and hips as you lower your glutes toward the floor (see figure *b*).

2. Keep your heels on the floor and back strong throughout the move.

3. Return to start and repeat single-leg squats with your right leg for the recommended number of reps.

4. Switch legs to complete a set.

b

Safety Tips

↘ Keep your abdominals engaged and back strong during this exercise.

↘ Try to push through the midfoot and heel of the foot that's balanced on the floor as you get into a squat and return to stand.

Training Tip

The single-leg squat is another good warm-up and body preparation exercise for leg work and running.

SQUAT ON A BALANCE MAT

Primary Muscles Worked

Hamstrings, glutes, calves, quads, and hip flexors

Equipment Needed

Balance mat, pillow, BOSU, or similar unsteady surface

Start

Stand tall with abdominals engaged and feet hip-width apart on a balance mat, pillow, or similar unsteady surface (see figure *a*).

Move

1. Get into a squat while keeping your balance (see figure *b*).
2. Bend at the hip and lower the glutes toward the floor.
3. Return to start and do recommended number of reps.

Training Tip

To improve your balance, you can try other standing exercises on a balance mat or other unsteady surface.

a

b

PLANK

Primary Muscles Worked

Abdominals, obliques, shoulders, and hips; with progression: hip flexors and extensors, quadriceps, adductors, and abductors

Equipment Needed

Mat (optional)

Start

1. Get into a bent-elbow plank with your forearms and toes on the floor or mat (see figure).
2. Engage your abdominal and gluteal muscles to hold your weight.

Move

Hold the plank for 30 seconds.

Variation: Plank With Knee Tuck

1. For the move segment, bend and rotate your right knee out and tuck your right knee in toward your right elbow.

2. Return to start and alternate legs for recommended number of reps.

Safety Tips

❯ Be mindful of your form, especially with the progression knee tucks. As you get tired, your hips may drop or rise.

❯ Keep your back straight, core engaged (squeeze the abdominal and gluteal muscles), and pelvis tucked under in order to keep your hips squared to the floor.

SUPERMAN

Primary Muscles Worked

Back, glutes, and hip extensors

Start

Lie facedown on a mat (optional) with arms extended so that they are parallel to your ears (see figure *a*).

Move

1. Squeeze the glutes and shoulder blades to lift your legs and torso off the floor slightly (see figure *b*).

2. Hold for one second. Return to start.

3. Do recommended number of reps.

Variation

You can extend your arms straight out to the side so that your upper body forms a T. If you have a history of neck pain, you may prefer this modification.

a

b

Safety Tip

Squeeze the shoulder blades and glutes throughout this exercise.

BIRD DOG (QUADRUPED)

Primary Muscles Worked

Abdominals, obliques, shoulders, and hips

Start

Get onto all fours with your shoulders over your hands and knees in line with the hips. Keep your back flat (see figure *a*).

a

Move

1. Use the core to lift the left arm so that it's parallel to your ears and extend the right leg behind you (see figure *b*).
2. Hold for one second. Return to start.
3. Switch sides.
4. Do recommended number of reps.

Safety Tip

Keep your back strong, but do not round your back during this exercise.

b

Coordination and Agility Exercises

The following exercises will help you work specific muscles required for performing movements that call on your coordination and agility, such as crawling and landing properly.

BEAR CRAWL

Primary Muscles Worked

Abdominals, obliques, shoulders, hip flexors, and extensors

Start

1. Get onto all fours with your shoulders over your hands and knees in line with the hips (see figure *a*).
2. Keep your back flat.
3. Use the core to lift your knees off the floor.

a

Move

1. Walk your body forward by moving the opposite arm and foot forward while keeping your knees bent (see figure *b*).

2. Alternate arms and legs until you've moved 10 feet forward. Then move backward, alternating the opposite arm and foot until you've reached where you started the exercise (see figure *c*).

3. Do recommended number of reps.

Variation

You can also do this exercise diagonally and laterally using the same mechanics (by alternating moving the opposite arm and leg simultaneously).

Safety Tip

Keep your back strong and core engaged, and try to keep your back straight throughout the exercise.

b

c

Training Tip

The bear crawl also helps with body control and is a great preparatory exercise for strength training.

SEAL WALK

Primary Muscles Worked

Abdominals, obliques, shoulders, hip flexors, and extensors

Equipment Needed

5- or 10-pound (2.5-5 kg) plate, sliding disc, ab roller, or paper plate

Start

a

1. Get into a straight-arm plank (the up part of a push-up) with your abdominal muscles engaged and pelvis tucked under.

2. Place a 5-pound (2.5 kg) plate, sliding disc, paper plate, or other sliding object on the floor under your toes (see figure *a*).

Move

1. Walk your body forward by moving your arms forward and sliding your feet along (see figure *b*).

b

(continued)

SEAL WALK *(continued)*

2. Move 5 to 10 feet (1.5-3 m) forward.

3. Then move backward, alternating arms until you've reached where you started the exercise (see figure *c*).

4. Do recommended number of reps.

Variation

You can do this exercise with your lower body (from the waist down) on the floor as you build up shoulder and forearm strength.

c

Safety Tip

Keep your back strong and core engaged and try to keep your back straight throughout the exercise.

Training Tip

The seal walk doubles as a shoulder mobility and strength exercise and helps with body control. It's a great preparatory exercise for strength training.

LANDING MECHANICS

Not an exercise all by itself, proper landing mechanics is something you'll need for your training and on race day. You can work on your landing form with jumps (see figure *a*), hops, and burpees. Use the following guidelines for sound landing form.

Primary Muscles Worked

Calves, quadriceps, hip flexors, and hamstrings

Move

1. Keep your knees slightly bent upon landing from a jump (see figure *b*).

2. Land from the ball of the foot to midfoot and heel so that your legs uniformly absorb the shock of the jump. This takes practice.

3. Keep proper landing mechanics in mind when you do any jump exercises coupled with a stand upon landing, such as burpees (with jumps) and single-leg hops.

a

b

Other Flexibility Exercises

The following exercises will help you delay muscle soreness and increase range of motion. You'll use them during the cool-down segments of a workout. If you have experience with yoga, it can be a beneficial way to improve your flexibility and reduce the chances of injury.

STANDING CHEST STRETCH

Primary Muscles Worked

Chest and anterior shoulders

Equipment Needed

Doorway

Start

1. Stand tall facing a doorway.
2. Outstretch your arms and hold on to either side of the doorway.

Move

1. Lean in until you feel a stretch in your chest and arms.
2. Hold for 30 seconds.

STANDING QUAD STRETCH

Primary Muscles Worked

Quadriceps

Start

Stand tall with your core engaged.

Move

1. Lift your right ankle toward your right glute.
2. Clasp your right ankle with your right hand (see figure). Hold stretch for 20 seconds.
3. Switch legs and repeat.

Training Tip

Throughout this stretch, keep the thighs parallel and close to each other.

STANDING CALF STRETCH

Primary Muscles Worked

Calves

Start

Stand tall with your core engaged about an arm's-length away from a wall and hands against the wall.

Move

1. Place the left foot forward, bend the knee of the left leg, and lean in slightly to feel a stretch in the right lower leg.
2. Hold stretch for 30 seconds.
3. Switch legs and repeat.

Variation

To stretch out the soleus (lower calf), bend the knee of the back leg slightly.

STANDING MID- AND UPPER-BACK STRETCH

Primary Muscles Worked

Mid- and upper back

Equipment Needed

Doorway

Start

Stand tall with your core engaged, an inch or two away from the side of a doorway.

Move

1. Walk your right arm up the doorway until it's straight, and lean in slightly.
2. Hold for 30 seconds.
3. Switch arms and repeat.

STANDING HAMSTRING STRETCH

Primary Muscles Worked

Hamstrings

Start

Stand tall with your hands by your sides.

Move

1. Bend and reach toward the floor until you feel a stretch in the backs of your legs. Try to keep your legs straight as you reach towards the floor (see figure).
2. Once you feel a stretch, hold for 30 seconds.

Safety Tip

To get out of this stretch, roll up slowly to a stand, especially if you have a tight or weak back.

KNEELING HIP FLEXOR STRETCH

Primary Muscles Worked

Hip flexors and quadriceps

Equipment Needed

Mat or pillow (optional)

Start

1. Get into a split kneeling position on a mat or other soft surface (pillow or outdoors on the grass).
2. Your right knee should be on the mat while your left leg is in front of you with the left knee bent so that it's over the left foot, which is on the floor (see figure *a*).

a

Move

1. Tuck the pelvis forward. You should feel a stretch in the quadriceps and hip flexors of the right leg.
2. Hold for 30 seconds.
3. Switch sides and repeat.

(continued)

KNEELING HIP FLEXOR STRETCH (continued)

Variation

If you don't feel a stretch in the right quadriceps or hip flexors, extend the right arm to reach to the ceiling and lean over to your left slightly (see figure b). This will also extend the stretch into your right side, including the lats and obliques.

b

FOREARM STRETCH

Primary Muscles Worked

Forearms

Start

Extend your left arm in front of you with your palm facing up.

a

Move

1. Use the right hand to bend your left hand at the wrist downward until you feel a stretch in the forearm (see figure a).

2. Hold for 20 seconds.

3. Then use your right hand to bend your left hand at the wrist upward as you bend your arm until you feel a stretch (see figure b).

4. Hold for 20 seconds.

5. Switch hands and repeat.

b

GLUTE STRETCH

Primary Muscles Worked

Glutes

Start

Sit on floor.

Move

1. Cross your right ankle over your left knee.
2. Twist and rest the back of your left elbow on the outside of your right knee (see figure).
3. Hold for 20 seconds.
4. Switch legs and repeat.

ADDUCTOR STRETCH

Primary Muscles Worked

Adductors, hips, and back

Equipment Needed

Mat or other soft surface

Start

Sit on the mat so that your knees are bent and your heels touch.

Move

Lean and reach forward toward the floor in front of you until you feel a stretch in the adductors (inner thighs, see figure).

CHILD'S POSE STRETCH

Primary Muscles Worked

Back

Equipment Needed

Mat or other soft surface

Start

Kneel on a mat with glutes resting on your heels.

Move

1. Crawl both hands forward while trying to keep your glutes on your heels (see figure). You should feel a stretch in your back and arms.
2. Hold for 20 seconds.

Postrace Recovery Mobility: Foam Rolling

Sometimes after a demanding obstacle race, your body can take a beating. The following exercises will simulate the benefits of a deep-tissue massage. Using a foam roller, you'll knead and release tight and sore muscles. Pay attention to large muscle groups such as your quads and hamstrings when working to recover heavily used muscles.

FOAM ROLL: GLUTES AND PIRIFORMIS

Primary Muscles Worked

Glutes and piriformis

Equipment Needed

Foam roller

Start

Sit on the foam roller with both knees bent.

Move

1. Cross your right ankle over your left knee and lean toward your right side (see figure).
2. Roll the length of the gluteal muscles on the right side, looking for tender spots.
3. Hold each tender spot for 20 seconds.
4. Repeat on other side.

FOAM ROLL: IT BAND AND ABDUCTOR

Primary Muscles Worked

IT band and abductors

Equipment Needed

Foam roller

Start

Lie on your right side so that the foam roller is 1 inch (2.5 cm) above the outside of your right knee.

Move

1. Roll the length of the IT bands and abductors from an inch or so above the outside of your right knee to just below the hip bone (see figure).
2. Hold each tender spot for 20 seconds.
3. Repeat on other side.

FOAM ROLL: ADDUCTOR

Primary Muscles Worked

Adductors

Equipment Needed

Foam roller

Start

Lie facedown in a bent-elbow plank position with the foam roller parallel to your body.

Move

1. Bend your left leg in toward your hip and out so that the inside of your left knee is resting on the foam roller.
2. Roll the length of the adductors from the inside of your left knee toward the groin area (see figure).
3. Hold each tender spot for 20 seconds.
4. Repeat on other side.

FOAM ROLL: CALF

Primary Muscles Worked

Calves

Equipment Needed

Foam roller

Start

Sit up with your legs straight.

Move

1. Cross your right ankle over your left ankle
   and rest the bottom half of your calf muscle (right above the Achilles) against the
   foam roller (see figure).

2. Roll the length of your calf muscle from above the Achilles to a few inches below the
   back of your right knee.

3. Hold each tender spot for 20 seconds.

4. Repeat on other side.

Final Thoughts

Mobility and balance are important aspects of obstacle race training
and preparation. We have covered more than 30 exercises that will help
you improve your mobility and balance. Upcoming chapters show you
how to put it all together for a training program that will help you crush
your obstacle race.

8

Power
and Strength

After a mile into his first race, Chris just didn't have the power and strength to climb walls and flip tires without help from fellow racers. Instead of running the hills, he had to walk, and it felt like his feet sank into the mud with each step. Chris needs to work on his power and strength to get through hills, walls, and similar challenges.

Building power and strength is essential for success in an obstacle race. You'll need power to carry logs, sandbags, and other large objects. You'll need it to flip tires; pull yourself over large walls; and drag heavy, cumbersome items. And, of course, you'll need strength to climb the steep hills and mountains, because running ability alone will not be enough to get you through the tough, grinding climbs.

To build power and strength specifically for obstacle racing, you'll need to determine what you need the power for. However, certain exercises are just beneficial to you overall. Many of these exercises involve lifting weights, but often power can also be developed simply by performing explosive movements. When lifting for power, you should perform exercises in sets for 2 to 6 repetitions (reps) at a time with rest periods of 1 to 5 minutes. In power training, you'll typically do 3 to 5 sets of an exercise. You can increase the weight once you've noticed that the muscles an exercise engages no longer feel fatigued after 3 to 5 sets of 6 reps.

Principles of Power and Strength Training

If you recall from chapter 5, power and strength require maximal effort and explosive movement. You need to abide by several principles when training for power and strength. Many help you maximize results, and many are simply for your own safety. When training to improve maximal effort and explosiveness, you are at a greater risk of injury simply because your body is being placed under a great deal of stress. Muscles and tendons are at their greatest risk of injury during power and strength training, particularly when training involves heavy weights. But if you train smart, don't overdo it, and follow these steps to mitigate risk, power training will be massively useful in your athletic development.

➘ **Always warm up first.** This means loosening up the muscles, performing dynamic warm-up exercises, and starting with lighter weights and gradually increasing the weights.

➘ **Increase weight in small increments.** It's easy to get caught up in strength gains. Make sure you develop at a reasonable rate. Increase the weight only by about 10 to 20 percent on each set, and increase maximum weight by no more than 10 percent per week.

➘ **Increase work volume increases for no more than three consecutive weeks.** Weight on specific lifts can increase for a total of three weeks in a row. After three weeks, you should scale back in weight and allow your body to recover, rebuild, and prepare for an increase the following week.

➘ **Be disciplined enough to avoid power training when extremely fatigued.** This one is self-explanatory. Do power training only if you are fresh enough to maintain form. If form begins to break down because of fatigue, cease power training immediately.

Power and Strength Training Techniques

There are a several ways to train for power with weights. When performing sets for maximal power and strength using any of these techniques, look to add a recovery time somewhere in the realm of 2 to 5 minutes between sets. This offers you a complete refueling of your energy stores between each set.

5x5 Weight Training

Complete lifts in sets of 5 reps. The goal is to lift close to your maximal strength for 5 sets of 5 reps on each exercise. This can be altered to 3 to 6 reps with a slight variance in weight.

Plyometric Training

Not all power needs to be developed with the use of weight training. Jumping, sprinting, and plyometrics are a great way to develop explosiveness without using weights. Plyometrics, often called plyo for short, are explosive movements often using just body weight. Plyo push-ups, lunge jumps, box jumps, and bounds are popular plyometric exercises you can use to increase explosiveness while improving landing mechanics at the same time.

Want to spice up your plyometric training? You can add weight to optimize results. Weight vests and sandbags are the best way to take your plyometric training to the next level. Load-bearing explosive movements can be even more beneficial once you have mastered form using your own body weight.

Uphill Sprinting

Very few activities engage the calves and glutes like a good uphill sprint. There are several varieties, but in this instance, shorter, more explosive runs are the key. These will improve your running power and ability to climb brutal hills on race day. And uphill sprints will make you faster! Sprints can be of a variety of distances. Previously we introduced hill repeats for the development of muscular and cardiorespiratory endurance. For the development of power, we want to shorten these runs. Explosive sprints ranging from 2 to 25 seconds will increase your power. Look for steep hills, along the lines of 10 to 40 percent incline. Try doing these runs on a treadmill if necessary, but your shorter runs will be much better and safer on a hill outdoors.

If you perform a run in the 2- to 4-second range, you are working on first-step speed: pure, raw, and explosive. This will generate pure strength gains. A run of 10 to 25 seconds will train your body to maintain speed over time.

Key Lifts for Power and Strength

Although you can use a variety of exercises and training tools to improve your power and strength, a few key moves form the foun-

OCR-SPECIFIC EQUIPMENT FOR POWER AND STRENGTH TRAINING

We always preach training for the situation you will encounter—the principle of specificity. Obstacle racing requires a great deal of power in various fashions during a race. So, train for those obstacles. You can use affordable training tools that can be built from supplies purchased at any hardware store. Cinder blocks, buckets of rocks, even tires—there's no shortage of creative ways to simulate race-day conditions and develop the power necessary for obstacle completion.

dation of power and strength training for obstacle racing. Early on in your training, you'll work on these key exercises: deadlift, squat, lunge, swing, and clean. Before discussing the correct form for each move, let's go over the benefits of these key exercises, starting with the deadlift.

The deadlift is one of the best exercises for developing strength in the glutes and hamstrings. It can also benefit your lower back. The deadlift requires you to generate force by driving your hips forward and engaging your hips, butt, and hamstrings. One thing that many people forget is that the gluteal muscles (butt) are the most powerful muscles in the leg, and most people do not take the time to develop them. Deadlifts not only help you increase the strength in your legs, but they also teach you to engage your glutes, taking the strain off your hamstrings during uphill climbing and allowing you to be more explosive. The deadlift should be a staple in your routine.

Like the deadlift, the squat is a great exercise for generating power in the quads as well as the glutes. With many variations, the squat allows your body to support a large load of weight with a stable movement. The squat adds a great deal of core strength in addition to leg strength because it forces your body to stabilize your spine by using your lower back and abdominal muscles. You can perform squats at their heaviest with the back squat (a bar across your back), but you can also perform them in manners more conducive to obstacle racing. These methods include the front squat and hang squat, the latter of which is performed with dumbbells.

The lunge, another lower-body exercise, can develop power as well as endurance. Variations allow you to increase strength as well as explosiveness. When weighted, the lunge can dramatically increase your power. Weighted walking lunges, jumping split lunges, and weighted split squats (which technically are not lunges but maintain a lunge position) all can increase your strength significantly. Jumping split lunges, in particular, help you work on power as well.

There are very few ways to develop power in the hamstrings. The deadlift is one way but can place a lot of pressure on your back if performed incorrectly or with weights that are too heavy. A good alternative is the kettlebell swing, which, when mastered, can develop explosive strength in the hamstrings and glutes while not placing as much strain on the back and can also engage your core and grip strength. For our purposes, we recommend the Russian kettlebell swing because it is easier on the shoulders than the American variety.

The power clean is one of the most effective full-body power training tools but also one of the more risky in terms of potential harm to the body, so perform cleans only under the close supervision of experienced professionals or if you are certain your technique is proper.

Now that you are familiar with the benefits of the key lifts for power and strength, let's discuss proper form, starting with the deadlift.

DEADLIFT

Primary Muscles Worked

Hip flexors, quadriceps, glutes, hamstrings

Equipment Needed

Dumbbells or barbell

Start

1. Stand tall with your abdominals engaged, back straight, and feet at least shoulder-width apart.

2. Hold a barbell or dumbbells at about midthigh height (see figure *a*).

3. Keep your shoulders back, chest out, and back flat. (When performing a deadlift, it is important to remember to use correct posture.)

Move

1. Drive your hips back to lower the weight down (see figure *b*).

2. Drive your hips forward to lift the weight back up to start.

3. Your glutes should be tight the entire time.

a

b

SQUAT

Primary Muscles Worked

Hip flexors, quadriceps, glutes, hamstrings

Start

1. Stand tall with your abdominals engaged, back straight, and feet about hip-width apart.
2. Hold a barbell at about midthigh height or dumbbells by your side in a hang carry (see figure *a*).
3. During a squat, the same principles of posture apply as with the deadlift. Keep your shoulders back, chest out, and back flat.

Move

1. With the chest out and shoulders back, press the hips back before descending.
2. Drop your butt low, creating a 90-degree angle at the back of the knees without allowing your shoulders to pull forward (see figure *b*).
3. Drive the hips back under you to return to start.

Variation: Thruster

Want to get even more out of the squat? Try the thruster, which adds an overhead press to the squat.

Start

1. Stand tall with the abdominals engaged, back straight, and feet hip-width apart.
2. Hold the barbell using a shoulder carry (right above chest height).

Move

1. With the chest out and shoulders back, press the hips back before descending,
2. Drop your butt low, creating a 90-degree angle at the back of the knees without allowing your shoulders to pull forward.
3. At the bottom of the front squat, the weight should still be held in a shoulder carry (see figure *c*). Do your best not to let the weight drift outward or downward.

a

b

c

(continued)

SQUAT *(continued)*

4. Drive the weight up over your head as you straighten the legs (see figure *d*), using the power of your legs for momentum.

5. Slowly return to start by lowering the weight to a shoulder carry.

Training Tip

A tight, engaged core is absolutely necessary for maintaining form.

d

LUNGE

Primary Muscles Worked

Quadriceps, hamstrings, glutes, calves

Start

1. Stand in a long, staggered stance.

2. Throughout the exercise, remember to keep your torso tall and vertical, preventing your shoulders from pulling forward.

Move

a

1. Bend the back knee and lower it toward the floor (see figure *a*). Your hips should lower but your posture remains tall.

2. Return to start by driving through your front foot and off your back toe (see figure *b*).

Training Tip

On any stationary lunge you will switch your feet by walking either your back foot forward or your front foot backward, depending on the specific lunge you are performing. Repeat by switching legs (see figure *c*).

b

Variation: Lunge Jump

1. To intensify this move and work on power, try the jumping switch lunge, which can be completed with or without dumbbells.

2. Explode off your front foot and off your toes, leaving the floor and switching your lead foot.

3. Land in a lunge position and gently lower yourself again.

c

KETTLEBELL SWING

Primary Muscles Worked

Quadriceps, hamstrings, glutes, hips, core, arms

Equipment Needed

Kettlebell

Start

1. Begin with the weight on the floor 12 to 18 inches (30-45 cm) out in front of you.

2. Stand with bent knees, back flat, chest out, and shoulders back.

3. Grab the bell loosely around the top of the handle.

a

Move

1. As you lift the weight, it will swing back between your legs (see figure *a*).

2. As your forearms and wrists press against your hips and thighs, thrust your hips forward with power, projecting your arms upward and driving the weight up to eye level (see figure *b*).

3. Squeeze your butt as you drive your hips forward. It will reach its apex there, then descend back between your legs.

4. Allow the weight to swing back as far as it will, engaging your core to keep it from pulling you too far forward.

5. Thrust your hips forward to repeat.

b

(continued)

KETTLEBELL SWING (continued)

Training Tips

1. Grip the weight loosely at the beginning and end of each swing and firmly though the middle.

2. For this exercise, try to keep your weight on your heels instead of the balls of your feet so you can stay anchored and keep your balance.

Variation: Single-Arm Kettlebell Swing

This progression is essentially the same, just with a single arm holding on to the kettlebell (see figures *c* and *d*). The single-arm swing allows you to improve grip strength and add variation through alternating arms and modified resistance.

c

d

POWER CLEAN

Primary Muscles Worked

Quadriceps, hamstrings, glutes, hips, core, arms

Equipment Needed

Barbell or dumbbells

Start

1. Stand tall with the abdominals engaged and the back strong.

2. Hold the bar or dumbbells in a hang-carry position, gripping the bar just wider than shoulder-width apart and with knees slightly bent. The bar or dumbbells should ideally hang just above the knees (see figure a).

a

Move

1. Drive the shoulders up and drive your legs straight. Your legs will push so hard you will literally leave the floor. As you do so, pull the elbows up and out to the sides (see figure b).

2. As the bar or dumbbells rise, drop under it by bending your knees and drive your elbows forward so that you hold the bar or dumbbells in the front squat position with torso tall (see figure c). If using a barbell, keep the elbows forward and wrists bent backward toward your body. Keep the weight close to your body the entire way up.

3. To return the weight back down, simply bend the knees and roll the elbows backward.

b

Tip

Throughout this exercise, maintain control of the weight. Start with a lighter weight, if necessary, until you feel comfortable with the form.

c

Final Thoughts

Power and strength are two of the most critical components of training for an obstacle race, but those new to the sport often overlook these aspects. Training to achieve and improve on your maximal effort and explosiveness isn't easy and can be risky when you use incorrect form. Follow the instructions for key lifts and other power and strength training techniques to ensure you get the most out of each exercise and minimize the risk of injury. When in doubt, consult with a qualified fitness professional to ensure you use proper form.

9

Grip Strength

Chris always thought he had pretty decent grip strength, but he really struggled with holding on to buckets and sandbags and even supporting his own weight on ropes and walls. He figured biceps curls would pretty much address forearm strength, but he didn't realize there's more to improving grip strength for obstacle racing. He'd like to include more relevant grip strength exercises in his training program.

Grip strength is a make-or-break skill set for many competitors in obstacle races. Often, the obstacles requiring major amounts of grip strength are some of the most complex, as well as some of the most fun and memorable of all the obstacles you will encounter during a race. Over the course of this chapter, you will be introduced to the three types of grip strength, their benefits, and ways to train the body to improve each of them.

Three Types of Grip Strength

There are three kinds of grip strength. Each has use in improving your performance in OCR events.

1. Crush grip: The grip between your fingers and your palm (used in rope climbs, monkey bars, cargo nets, and hoist obstacles)

2. Support grip: A static grip that involves maintaining a grip or hold for a long period of time (jerry can carries, bucket carries, farmer's carries, and heavy drags)

3. Pinch grip: The grip between your fingers and your thumb (wall traverses, throwing challenges, and some sandbag carries)

Each type of grip strength can be used in an obstacle race. The greatest emphasis in training should be placed on the crush grip and the support grip, since the pinch grip is not required as often in order to master obstacles.

Warm-Up

Before training for grip strength, you need to warm up properly. This means loosening the entire body, specifically focusing on loosening the muscles of the fingers, forearms, and biceps.

Dynamic Stretches

1. Swing the arms in each plane of motion (up and down, front and back, side to side) to prepare the shoulders and biceps.

2. Get the blood flowing a bit with 6 to 10 push-ups.

3. Clench and unclench the hands to get the forearms and fingers ready for grip strength training.

4. Rotate the wrists to limber up the joints and forearm muscles.

5. Stretch each wrist by briefly pulling the the fingertips of your hand up and then down until you feel tension in the wrist and forearms.

Static Stretches

1. The most effective of forearm stretches involves facing your palms upward, pulling downward on your fingers using the opposite hand, and then driving your elbow upward. This move is comparable to the dynamic stretch in step 5, but instead of briefly pulling on your fingertips, you hold the stretch. Alternate numerous times on each wrist, holding for 20 seconds each time.

2. You can also stretch the exterior of the forearm by pulling your hand inward toward the interior of the wrist. Just pull very lightly to avoid injury.

Once you've finished warming up, you can begin to work on your grip strength.

Training for Crush Grip

Crush grip is probably the most important form of grip strength for obstacle racing. Keep in mind that crush grip is the ability to squeeze something between your fingers and palm. There are many ways to train for crush grip. The following are a few you'll see in this program.

HAND CLENCH

Equipment Needed

Tennis ball

Start

Sit or stand tall with your hands in front of you.

Move

Clench your hands while squeezing a tennis ball and release them (see figure *a*). Do this at least 8-10 times as part of a warm-up prior to a grip strength-focused workout.

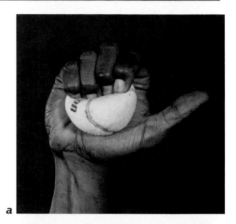

a

Training Tip

Doing hand clenches 50 to 100 times each morning is a simple way to improve grip strength.

Variations

Clench and crumple a sheet of newspaper in each hand and squeeze it for the recommended number of reps. You can also use only two fingers rather than your entire hand (see figure *b*). You can also use stress balls or a tennis ball to enhance your crush grip; you can squeeze these using the same motion as you would use for hand clenches.

b

GRIP CLENCH

Equipment Needed

Spring-loaded grip strengthener

Start

Sit or stand tall, holding on to a spring-loaded grip strengthener in each hand. (You can also do one hand at a time if you have only one grip strengthener.)

Move

1. Clench your hands to squeeze the grip strengthener as much as you can (see figure *a*).

2. Hold the squeeze momentarily (see figure *b*) and release.

3. Repeat for 5-8 reps.

Training Tip

Keep a spring-loaded grip strengthener in the car and use it while sitting in traffic; it both boosts your strength and allows you to release some frustration!

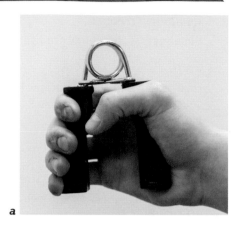

a

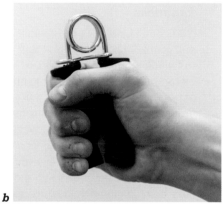

b

ROPE CLIMB

Equipment Needed

Rope secured to a sturdy overhead attachment

Start

Hold on to a rope firmly with both hands, using a secure grip (see figure *a*). Hold the rope between both feet (see figure *b*).

Move

Move up the rope as far as you can with a good grip, alternating hands and feet. Work up to climbing at least 10 feet (3 meters) high and work your way down while maintaining a secure grip.

a

Variations

If you don't have the grip or upper-body strength to pull yourself up the rope or if your grip is starting to fatigue after climbing a foot or two (0.3-0.6 meters), simply try to hold on to the rope as long as you can. Even if you can't pull yourself up the group, try to lift your feet off the ground so you can practice supporting your weight using your grip strength, even if it's only for a few seconds. Work up to a minute and once you've reached that milestone, practice moving up and down the rope. Even just hanging from the rope can enhance grip strength so that when you encounter a rope late in a race, you won't have any problems with clinging on and scampering up it.

b

Safety Tip

If you are afraid of heights or if grip strength is a particular weakness for you, be sure to have cushy mats/padding at the base of the rope and consider asking having a friend or fitness professional to help spot you as you work your way up and down the rope.

Training Tip

Practicing rope climbs is another great way to work on your crush grip and also your support grip. Climbing ropes, particularly without the use of your legs, will improve not only your grip but also your overall strength in your arms and back.

TOWEL PULL-UP

Equipment Needed

Pull-up bar and towel (or two)

Start

Hang the towel over a bar. If you are using one towel, hold one end of the towel in each hand. If you use two towels, hang the towels over opposite ends of the bar so you can grip the ends of each towel with either hand (i.e., each towel essentially forms a handle).

Start

1. Grab the towel using a crush grip (see figure a).

2. Retract your shoulders to activate your upper-back muscles.

a

Move

1. Lift yourself up as you would for a regular pull-up (see figure b).

2. Practice as many pull-ups as you can this way, squeezing the towel between your hands. For beginners, this may be a half a rep. For inter-mediate-advanced exercises, try to do at least 10-12 reps of towel pull-ups.

Training Tip

One of the most functional ways to train your crush grip is to use a towel to perform pull-ups. You can also practice hanging in this manner to enhance the strength in your fingers, hands, and forearms.

b

ALTERNATIVE WAYS TO IMPROVE GRIP STRENGTH

Heading to your local playground is another simple way to improve your grip strength. Things that came naturally to you as a child, including playing on the monkey bars, swinging from the chain rings, and climbing up and down the poles, are no longer so simple. Performing "workouts" on a local jungle gym can do wonders for preparing your body for the rigors of advanced obstacles, and your grip strength will be rewarded. It will also advance your skills from a race perspective. Practice navigating monkey bars and chain rings, sometimes with sets of pull-ups built in. Practice forward and backward, because you might find navigating certain obstacles where you're hanging from your hands can often be made easier by traveling backward. It can take a bit of the pressure off of your fingers, biceps, and shoulders.

Fat grips and globe grips are another excellent way to build crush grip strength. These items are slipped over a barbell and provide a difficult surface to grip as you lift weights. This can vastly improve your grip as you struggle to hold on to the minimalist grips. This is a simple tool you can use during your strength-focused workouts.

Training for Support Grip

As you recall, support grip is the ability of your fingers and forearms to support weight for an extended period. Some obstacles may call on both crush and support grip. For example, heavy carries and drags require both crush and support grip strength. You can train your support grip in several ways, both through basic strength training and through race simulation training.

Some forms of strength training are very efficient at improving grip strength in addition to other forms of strength. Kettlebell swings, which are introduced in chapter 6, are a perfect example. If you have solid form, try doing 2 minutes of kettlebell swings and see how quickly your arms fatigue. Your fingers, hands, and forearms will be tremendously tested as you get all the other benefits of a kettlebell swing simultaneously.

As with many other forms of strength, event simulation training is often the most effective. Following are a few techniques you can use to train specifically for obstacles that require support grip strength.

SUPPORT HANG

One of the simplest ways to train your support grip in a gym is by using a simple pull-up bar or suspension straps. You can use the straps or pull-up bar to simply hang.

Equipment Needed

Pull-up bar or suspension straps

Start

1. Hold on to the pull-up bar, towel, or suspension straps (see figures *a* and *b*).

2. Make sure your shoulders are retracted so that you are also engaging your upper-back muscles.

a

b

Move

Hang on for as long as you can. Beginners may start with straight-arm hangs, while more advanced exercisers may hang with both elbows bent (see figures *c* and *d*). If you are a beginner, try to hold on for at least a minute. You can also work up to a minute-hold, but holding on in increments of 15-30 seconds. Intermediate-advanced exercisers can experiment with the straight-arm or elbow-bent hang, working up to a two-minute hold.

Variations

↘ On the pull-up bar, try hanging on for as long as you can after doing pull-ups to exhaustion.

↘ Practice long holds at the bottom of each pull-up for as many repetitions as you can.

↘ Mixing it up but continually finding new ways to challenge your grip strength is the key. You can substitute a suspension inverted row or an inverted row hold in place of a pull-up at any time.

c

Training Tip

Whether these hangs use straight or bent arms, you will give your fingers, hands, and forearms the challenge you are looking for.

d

FARMER'S CARRY

The farmer's carry is one of the most common obstacles for support grip strength found in races. This could be in the form of a jerry can carry, two sandbags, or a variety of other items you might be required to carry at your sides across a distance. Train for these obstacles by simulating the race environment.

Equipment Needed

Jugs or pails filled with water (a gallon is approximately 8 pounds, so use your judgment when selecting a size)

Start

Stand tall with your core engaged and carry a water jug in each hand.

Move

1. Carry the water jugs as you walk forward for 100 yards at a time (see figure).

2. Return to start

Variations

❯ You can do the same simulation with kettlebells or large dumbbells.

❯ Practice going up and down hills and over uneven terrain to train more specifically for race conditions.

Training Tips

❯ This is great practice for your support (and crush) grip strength and will also strengthen other muscles as you compensate for the water sloshing around.

❯ The type of container you use—pail, jug, bucket, canister—will vary across races, so feel free to be creative and vary the type of receptacle you use with this exercise.

BUCKET CARRY

Some races will challenge you with a heavy bucket carry of some kind. That bucket might be full of rocks, sand, or gravel, and some might be full of water. Whatever the carry is, the best way to prepare your body for the rigors of this obstacle is to face it head on.

Equipment Needed

A 5-gallon bucket, usually available from your local hardware store. Fill it about 80 percent with gravel, sand, or even a heavy dumbbell. For women, try to fill it at least 60 percent.

Start

Try gripping the bucket with the fingers of one hand under the front of the bucket and the other hand gripping your wrist (see figure). (This way, your grip is locked in and the bucket is pinned closely to your chest; if you keep the bucket high on your hip, possibly even resting on your hip bone or your race belt, you can limit the damage to your grip strength, saving it for later obstacles.)

Move

Practice the bucket carry 50 to 300 yards at a time.

Safety Tip

You may find that the bucket weighs heavily on your fingers, forearms, and biceps. That's why we recommend using your off-hand to support your wrist, but it will take time and practice to build up the strength.

Training Tip

Mix up the terrain and practice going up and down hills.

Training for Pinch Grip

Pinch strength is a very specialized grip, ideal for bouldering and similar obstacles. Specifically, pinch grip engages the strength between your fingers and thumb. Practical training is always best, so getting out to a local rock climbing gym and practicing your holds are ideal. But if you don't have a bouldering wall available, here are other options at home or in the gym.

PINCH GRIP RAISE

Equipment Needed

Weighted plates, anywhere from 5 pounds (2.5 kg) all the way up to 45 (20 kg) per hand

Start

Stand or sit tall with good posture. Pinch a plate between your thumb and fingers (see figure *a*).

Move

Raise the plate up in front of you (see figure *b*), then lower it back down (see figure *c*).

Variations

You can also practice the same pinch grip with the weights hanging in front of you or at your sides. See how long you can maintain your grip.

a

b

c

PINCH GRIP TRANSFER

Equipment Needed

A weighted plate, anywhere from 5 pounds (2.5 kg) all the way up to 45 (20 kg)

Start

Stand tall with good posture. Pinch a plate between your thumb and fingers.

Move

1. Pass the plate between your hands (see figures *a* and *b*).

2. For the move part of this exercise, transfer the plate around your body or in a figure-eight pattern around and between your legs. Be sure to maintain a strong back for good form.

Training Tip

Pinch grip transfers allow for more dynamic training than raises and lifts.

a

b

PINCH GRIP SQUEEZE

Equipment Needed

Body weight only

Start

Stand or sit tall with your hands in front of you.

Move

1. Practice your pinch grip by squeezing your thumbs and hold for 1 second.

2. Release fingers and thumbs and repeat move 1 and move 2 for recommended reps.

Training Tip

Practicing this simple technique daily will gradually increase strength, power, and endurance in your fingers, hands, and forearms.

SANDBAG CARRY

Equipment Needed

Traditional sandbag, sandbell, or similar equipment in which you can grip with thumb and fingers

Start

Stand tall with core engaged and back strong. Place a sandbag or sandbell over your right shoulder.

Move

1. Reach over with your left hand and pinch the end of the bag to keep it in place (see figure *a*).

2. Walk with the sandbag over your shoulder for 300 to 500 yards (270-450 m).

3. Alternate shoulders and hands (see figure *b*) because the fatigue in your fingers and thumb will rapidly increase over the course of this exercise.

Variations

Sandbag Hike

Practice sandbag holds over the course of a hike, alternating shoulders and hands as needed.

Sandbag Squat

1. Hold the sandbag over one shoulder as you complete a set of squats.

2. Switch shoulders for the next set.

Training Tip

The beauty of this form of pinch grip training is that your legs and core build strength while you work on your grip.

General Forearm and Grip Strengthening

Strengthening all the muscles in your forearms will also enhance grip strength. There are countless ways to do so, but here are a few simple techniques you can do at home or in the gym.

WRIST CURL

The wrist curl improves forearm strength.

Primary Muscles Worked

Forearms and shoulders

Equipment Needed

Weighted barbell, weight plates (the bar can be loaded with either light weight or no weight at all), or dumbbells

Start

Hold the bar or dumbbell with palms facing forward (see figure *a*).

Move

Flex your wrist to curl the weight toward the ceiling (see figure *b*).

Training Tips

- To strengthen the outside of your forearm, grip the bar or dumbbell in front of you with palm facing toward you and arm straight.

- Extend your wrist by bringing the top of your hands toward the ceiling.

a

b

TOWEL TWIST

Probably the easiest way to improve grip and forearm strength with minimal effort is with towel twists.

Primary Muscles Worked

Forearms

Equipment Needed

A thick towel that you don't care about ruining

Start

Hold the towel with both hands.

Move

1. Practice twisting the towel over and over until it gets so tight it can no longer be twisted (see figure).

2. Practice twisting the towel in the other direction with the same result.

Training Tip

You can do this while watching TV or lying in bed, and it can make your hands, fingers, and forearms significantly stronger.

HEAVY TIRE FLIP

A fantastic way to develop grip strength is the heavy tire flip. It's difficult to have access to a heavy tire (over 100 pounds [45 kg], some as heavy as 400 pounds [180 kg]), but you have a couple options. You might find a heavy tire at a local junk yard. Or, if there's a high school football team nearby, it's often easy to access the ones left on the field after practices; just be sure you have permission to use them.

Equipment Needed

Heavy tire

Start

The heavy tire flip should begin very similar to your deadlift. Keep a flat back and start with your butt low (see figure *a*)

a

Move

1. Drive up through your heels, driving your hips forward in the process.

2. As the tire rises, walk forward, driving off your back foot and pushing the tire forward (see figure *b*).

Safety Tip

This can be a dangerous way to train, so be cautious not to throw your back into the lift or to let the tire fall on your fingers or toes.

b

WEIGHTED DRAG

Weighted drags can help improve your support grip. Dragging something heavy like a cinder block or heavy tire by a chain or rope will challenge both your grip strength and endurance. You will have to squeeze hard enough to maintain a solid grip and generate force as well as maintain grip endurance as you drag the object over a measured distance. The drags can be either short distance with heavier weights, such as large truck tires, or longer distances with slightly less weight. Either way, your support grip will be tested and improved.

Equipment Needed

Cinder block, large truck tire, sled, or weights, and a rope or chain.

Move

To do a high-quality drag, you can practice single-handed at your side or behind you (see figure a), double-handed at your side, or with the chain or rope pulled over and around the front of your hip (see figure b).

Training Tip

During a race, the chain or rope pulled over and around the front of your hip is the way you will ideally want to pull any item that must be dragged for a long distance. By pulling the chain or rope up and in front of you, you lift the front of the heavy object off the ground, eliminating friction and allowing it to move more easily, thus saving not just grip strength but also strength throughout your entire body.

a

b

Final Thoughts

Grip strength is often neglected in training. It's an important part of your OCR training, but that doesn't mean you need to devote entire training sessions to the skill. Try to work on it during training circuits, between circuit bouts, and in your spare time. No matter what you do to work on your grip strength, be aware that you should always warm up before and cool down after, including working on wrist and finger mobility as well as flexibility in the forearms through light stretching. You'll find that if you put in the time to develop your grip strength and master a few of the basic obstacles that it applies to, you will go a long way toward improving your race. Make yourself a well-rounded athlete and you'll be much more likely to succeed.

PART III
WORKOUTS AND TRAINING PLANS

10

Workouts

Now that he knows the demands of obstacle racing along with the exercises he needs to master for his next race, how does he put everything together into effective training sessions? Knowing that obstacle racing requires a balance of endurance, strength, flexibility, and power, Chris would like to know how to combine everything into sport-specific workouts.

We'll start with foundation and aerobic base building workouts, then move on to strength and lactate threshold training, and end with speed and power as well as skill development. Each phase lasts for a month, totaling 3 months for the entire program. You can access your specific daily training plan from the training calendars in chapter 11.

Running Workouts

This chapter presents running workouts that fit each phase of your training. The letters associated with the exercises correspond with some recommended training plans in chapter 11. Feel free to alter those recommendations with different exercises according to your needs. The number of repetitions you'll do in each workout will be based on the distance of the race you are training for. Short is 3 to 5 miles (5-8 km), intermediate is 6 to 9 miles (10-14 km), and long is 10 or more miles (16+ km).

All workouts require a warm-up and cool-down. Generally a 10- to 15-minute jog followed by about 6 to 10 striders (accelerations of 80-110 m) and some light stretching should suffice. Many of these workouts will require you to figure out your desired pacing. The concept of goal race pace is mentioned regularly. For more experienced runners, race pace will generally range from 10K to 10-mile race pace. This is because an obstacle race of 3 to 5 miles will be more taxing than a normal 3- to 5-mile running race, so your pace may be 10 to 20 percent slower, maybe even more so. If you're unsure, you'll have to go more off of perceived exertion levels. Race pace is a running speed that is too fast for you to converse much beyond a few words at a time. Your breathing will be labored, your legs will be burning, and you will be significantly challenged to maintain that pace for the entirety of the workout. Another simple way to look at a pace, such as a goal 5K pace, would be just a general pace you think you could maintain for approximately 20 to 25 minutes at maximum effort. A 10K pace is about 10 percent slower.

Phase 1: Foundation Running Workouts

Phase 1, your first month of training, is about setting the groundwork for the next 2 months. It's about laying the foundation by building basic strength and endurance. If you think you already have your desired base levels of strength and endurance, you can eliminate the first 2 weeks of phase 1 and accelerate the shift into phase 2. Following are a few workouts to aid in the development of your foundation.

A. Speed Play (Fartlek Training)

Originally a Swedish training technique, speed play workouts strengthen your running, teach your body to keep moving through fatigue, and train your body to change gears during your races. Several formats fall under the category of speed play. But the basic idea is that you never stop running during these workouts. Your pace is alternating between hard tempo and light jog. What follows are sequences based on the distance of the race you are preparing for. Be sure to repeat the entire sequence for the designated number of rounds. A round is a hard run with a jogging recovery.

> Short: Alternating 1-minute hard runs with 1-minute jogs (10 total rounds)
>
> Intermediate: 1-minute run, 1-minute jog, 2-minute run, 1-minute jog (5-8 total rounds)
>
> Long: 1-minute run, 1-minute jog, 2-minute run, 1-minute jog, 3-minute run, 1-minute jog (complete 5-10 total rounds)
>
> Long: 2 × 200 meters, 2 × 400 meters, 2 × 600 meters, 2 × 800 meters, 2 × 600 meters, 2 × 400 meters, 2 × 200 meters

Feel free to repeat the entire sequence or additional repetitions of the 800-meter interval.

B. Middle-Distance Hill Repeats

This workout will help you develop the ability to climb hills as well as maintain a higher-intensity output over time and build strength and endurance in your posterior chain, namely your glutes, hamstrings, and calves.

Find yourself a reasonably steep hill that will take you 1 to 3 minutes to run to the top of or run an equivalent amount of time on a treadmill. Incline can be anywhere from 4 to 10 percent incline. Run to the top of the hill at about 80 percent effort, and then jog back to the bottom. Repeat for a designated time. If you are on a treadmill, a light jog or walking recovery of half the time the run took you will suffice. Feel free to drop the incline for your recovery walk if you feel the need. As you repeat this workout further into your training, you may want to consider raising your incline to higher levels to continue to challenge yourself and improve.

Short: repeat for 20 minutes

Intermediate: repeat for 30 to 40 minutes

Long: repeat for 50+ minutes

C. Pace Shift Training

This workout is a slightly more advanced version of a fartlek session: continuous laps of a 400-meter track, alternating 200 meters (half a lap) at about your goal 5K pace, followed by 200 meters at about 10 to 15 seconds slower than the 200 you just ran. The 12 laps will maximize performance in a 5K race, so the number of laps needs to be adjusted accordingly depending on the distance of your race. Steve Prefontaine, who is considered the greatest runner in American history, used workouts like this in the 1970s on his way to American records in races of every distance from 2,000 meters to 10,000 meters.

Short: 10 to 12 laps

Intermediate: 16 to 20 laps

Long: 24+ laps

D. Stadium Training

Similar to hill training, these workouts boost strength and endurance simultaneously. Find a local stadium with either bleachers or a large number of steps. This workout is fairly simple. Run to the top of the steps, across to the next row, and back down.

Short: 20 minutes

Intermediate: 30 to 40 minutes

Long: 50 to 60+ minutes

E. Foundation Ladder Workout

The ladder workout is integrated into a variety of training programs and can vary based on your goals. Typically, the distances both ascend and descend over the course of the workout, but that isn't always a given. Essentially, you start by completing a series of runs at a set distance that will be indicated in your training plan. The runs gradually get longer until you reach the top of the ladder. Then they gradually get shorter until you reach the bottom again.

For this workout, try to do each repetition with only 1 minute of walking or jogging recovery in between. Perform the runs at 10 to 15 percent faster than goal race pace.

Short: 2 × 200 meters, 2 × 400 meters, 1 × 800 meters, 1 × 400 meters, 1 × 200 meters

Intermediate: 2 × 200 meters, 2 × 400 meters, 2 × 600 meters, 1 × 800 meters, 1 × 600 meters, 1 × 400 meters, 1 × 200 meters

Note: To add mobility and strength to this workout, complete all or portions of going down the stairs as a downward bear crawl. You'll do this move on the hands and feet, crawling down the stairs headfirst, so be careful.

Phase 2: Endurance and Lactate Threshold Running Workouts

In phase 2 of training, the goal is to boost endurance and lactate threshold by performing significantly more taxing routines. These routines include steeper hills, longer intervals, and uncomfortable tempos. Lactate threshold training teaches your body to resist the buildup of lactic acid, which in turn will allow you to run faster for a longer time. Lactic acid accumulates in the system, most notably in the legs, and causes them to feel heavy and to burn and fatigue. So improving your threshold can go a long way toward improving your racing ability.

A. 800-Meter Repeats

These runs increase your endurance, boost lactate threshold, and teach your body what your race pace will feel like once fatigued.

Find a local track. Run 800 meters (2 laps) at a pace 10 percent faster than goal race pace. Your recovery will be either a 400-meter light jog or a 200-meter walk. An additional option may be a 100-meter walk and a 300-meter jog. Try to hit the same time on each run.

Short: 4 rounds

Intermediate: 5 to 7 rounds

Long: 8 to 12 rounds

Note: You can do a very similar workout with 1,000-meter intervals as well, which will place even greater emphasis on lactic threshold and slightly less on speed.

B. Mile Repeats

The mile repeat is probably the most efficient way to develop endurance and stamina while also conducting race pace simulation. And it is one of the best ways to develop mental strength and confidence in your abilities.

The workout is as simple as it sounds. Complete your assigned number of 1-mile runs (4 laps on a track) or a similar loop elsewhere with minimal rest in between. Your goal is to run at or faster than your desired race pace. A pace that you can run for 25 to 35 minutes at maximum effort will suffice.

Short: 2 or 3 × 1 mile; recovery = 3-minute jog

Intermediate: 4 or 5 × 1 mile; recovery = 2-minute jog or 400-meter light jog

Long: 6+-mile intervals; recovery = 60 to 90 seconds, or a 100-meter jog out and 100-meter jog back

C. Long Hill Climbs

We're back to hill interval repeats, this time with some longer climbs. Again, the goal is lactic threshold and endurance building. So you need to focus on finding a hill that is longer than the one you used in your previous training phase and practice running up the hill numerous times in a training session. Your goal is to sustain consistent speed on each climb at a challenging threshold and to sustain those climbs for 3 to 5 minutes. Your recovery is the jog back down. If you don't have a hill long enough, use a treadmill, with 1:1 work-to-recovery ratio. You can walk or jog for your recovery. If you do this on a treadmill, select an incline of 5 to 15 percent; for recovery, opt for 1 to 2 minutes for recovery.

Short: 2 or 3 climbs

Intermediate: 4 to 7 climbs

Long: 8 to 12+ climbs

D. Running and Strength Combinations

A favorite training routine of mine is running intervals combined with strength, particularly leg strength, because there are so many ways to do so. Developing your ability to run while fatigued is a critical element of success in an obstacle race. One of the simplest ways to train is to combine running intervals at lactic threshold pace with lunges, which challenge your system anaerobically. If you're doing lunges as your strength between runs, the type of lunge can determine the ideal rep counts. For example, walking lunges can get rep counts that range from 30 to 100 per recovery. Because of their explosiveness, the jumping switch lunge involves lower rep counts, more along the lines of 20 to

40. With squats, the rep counts would be similar with 25 to 50 for a body-weight squat and lower counts of 10 to 25 reps for plyometric or heavier strength moves like weighted squats or squat jumps. Gradually raise your rep counts as you progress in your training.

Short: 8 × 400 meters or 6 × 600 meters at 80 percent effort with 30 to 50 walking lunges or body-weight squats as recovery. If you opt for switch lunges, squat jumps, or split squats, try 20 to 30 reps.

Intermediate: 10 × 600 meters or 8 × 800 meters at 80 percent effort with 40 to 70 walking lunges or body-weight squats in between. If you opt for switch lunges, squat jumps, or split squats, try 30+ reps.

Long: 12 × 800 meters or 10 × 1,000 meters at 80 percent effort with 60 to 80 walking lunges or body-weight squats. If you opt for switch lunges, squat jumps, or split squats, opt for 30 to 50 reps.

Phase 3: Speed, Explosiveness, and Fine Tuning

Phase 3 is about developing leg turnover, power, and explosiveness as well as sharpening some of the skills necessary for completing the more challenging races.

A. 200-Meter Repeats on Total Time

In this workout, your goal is to complete your intervals at a very high speed with a consistently minimal recovery time—essentially, sprints on very short recovery. You're working on leg turnover in addition to endurance and aerobic capacity. Each interval is 200 meters. You have 1 minute to complete your 200-meter run. Any remaining time in that minute is recovery and then you're right into your next interval. You should set a goal time for each 200-meter run. Alternatively, if you need to scale back your pace, you can opt to complete 30 to 40 seconds of sprinting instead of measuring for meters. At the end of each sprint, you can walk for however much time remains in that minute before beginning your next sprint. This workout is ideally done on a track for accurate measurements of your meters. Regardless of which format of the workout you select, you will be able to see how much ground you cover and how long it takes very accurately from a track. The key is consistency. If you are running exactly 200 meters, you will be able to measure the exact number of seconds it takes you. Your goal is to keep every split within a second or two. If your runs are based on time, see how much distance you cover on your first run, then try to reach or exceed that distance on each subsequent run over the same amount of time.

Short: 8 to 12 repeats

Intermediate: 16 to 20 intervals

Long: 24 to 32+ intervals

B. 400-Meter Repeats on Total Time

This workout is very similar to the previously mentioned 200-meter repeats. This time the distance of each interval is doubled to 400 meters. You will run 400 meters hard; similar to the previous workout, you will have 2 minutes to complete it and your recovery. At the end of those 2 minutes you resume running again.

Set a goal time for completing the runs. If you fail to complete any of those runs in your goal time or faster, the workout is immediately over, so consistency is key. The rules of the workout change slightly. While the 200s were about completing a large quantity of repetitions, this workout is about improvement. Your goal is to complete it on four consecutive weeks and note your improvement.

Short: 5 to 8 repeats

Intermediate: 10 to 15 repeats

Long: 16 to 20+ repeats

Note: If you need to ensure a slightly longer recovery, you can always do your runs for 70 to 80 seconds and recover the rest of the time. However, you will need to mark on a track or treadmill how far you made it and set a goal distance to cover.

C. Steep Hill Repeats

Steep hill sprints are about building power and explosiveness, particularly strength in your posterior chain (hamstrings, calves, and glutes), as well as your quads. So for this workout, find a truly challenging hill. It doesn't need to be long; 40 to 100 meters should suffice. Your goal is to run literally as fast as you possibly can to the top of the hill. Walk down for a recovery. Recovery should last about 90 seconds to 2 minutes. If completing the workout on a treadmill, you can pause and dismount, or just walk for recovery. Because these sprints are about exclusively raw strength speed and explosiveness, look for a hill that ranges from 10 to 20+ percent incline.

Short: 6 to 8 repeats

Intermediate: 10 to 15 repeats

Long: 16 to 20+ repeats

D. Heavy-Carry Running Repeats

One of the most effective ways to prepare your body for actual obstacle race simulation is a combination of strength and running with heavy carries. This will teach your body to shift gears and keep your feet moving as you encounter heavy strength obstacles and shift back to running.

You can opt to carry a bucket full of rocks, a sandbag, a log, or a tire, among other possible items. Choose a hill of moderate length and distance and alternate between running up and down it and then climbing it as quickly as you can while carrying your heavy object. Each carry should take 2 to 5 minutes.

Short: 4 to 6 repeats

Intermediate: 7 to 10 repeats

Long: 11 to 14+ repeats

Strength Workouts

Just as with running workouts, you must work through three phases of training for strength. Again, it begins with foundation, graduating to endurance, and finishing with power and explosiveness.

Phase 1: Foundation Strength Workouts

A foundation of strength is key to preparing for the upcoming routines and ensuring you don't injure yourself in future workouts. Building your strength phase by phase is the most proven method to a completely well-rounded fitness level.

A. Walking Lunge Repeats

One of the keys to success in obstacle racing is having leg strength that doesn't fade. A great way to build that strength and to simulate the fatigue those legs will feel is through lunge sets. Start with a small quantity in each set and gradually increase those reps. Go out for a set time, alternating between a specific number of walking lunges and a 60-second walk between sets. Start with counts of 30 lunges at a time and gradually work your way up to 100. Be aware this workout can make you incredibly sore, so be sure to cool down appropriately.

Short: 20 minutes

Intermediate: 30 minutes

Long: 45 to 60+ minutes

B. Pull/Push Workout

A great way to build strength and muscular endurance is to conduct a bodyweight circuit comprised of push and pull exercises pieced together in a way that allows you to continuously work for extended periods of time. Below is an example, where the rep counts rise as the exercises becomes more challenging.

5 pull-ups

10 push-ups

15 body-weight squats

Note: Substitute rows on a suspension device or inverted rows for the pull-ups if you struggle with pull-ups but still want to do this workout. Regardless of the distance you're training for, this workout is 20 minutes, but you can make it longer if you would prefer. See chapter 6 for instructions on executing pull-ups, push-ups, and body-weight squats.

C. Foundation Kettlebell Pyramid

This workout is a pyramid, meaning you start at a low rep count for each exercise and gradually increase your rep counts, peaking at the highest point, and then gradually reduce your rep counts. If you make it back to the bottom of the pyramid and time remains, work your way back up again.

The emphasis on kettlebell swings should always be on engaging your hamstrings and glutes. On thrusters it should be a full range of motion, squatting low and driving your hips back under you at the top while driving your arms all the way up. For instructions on executing these exercises, see chapter 8.

Kettlebell swing

Kettlebell thruster

Push-up

Rep counts: 6, 9, 12, 15, 12, 9, 6 . . .

Short: 6 to 7 minutes

Intermediate: 9 to 12 minutes

Long: 14 to 20 minutes

D. Foundation Pull-Up and Burpee Workout

This workout is an incredibly challenging routine that will test your lungs in addition to your upper-body and grip strength. You will follow a sequence of descending rep counts of pull-ups paired with ascending rep counts of burpees. There is no rest, and the goal is to complete the routine as quickly as possible. Mark your time and aim to beat it the next time you attempt the workout. Chapter 6 contains instructions on performing the following exercises. The workout is as follows:

10 pull-ups and 1 burpee

9 pull-ups and 2 burpees

8 pull-ups and 3 burpees

The sequence ends when you complete 1 pull-up and 10 burpees.

Note: If you can't do pull-ups, suspension-device rows are an appropriate substitute.

Phase 2: Strength Endurance Workouts

Once you've developed a fitness base, we can begin to work on your strength endurance, which is your ability to sustain a powerful physical effort over time.

A. Biceps and Grip Strength Endurance TOTM

Using nothing more than a suspension strap and a set of dumbbells, you can build unbelievable strength in your biceps and grip that you can sustain over time. You can use your preference of suspension device straps or dumbbells for your curls, but whichever you choose it has to be extremely challenging from the start when you hit the curls. Your biceps and grip strength will be tested and you may reach the point of extreme muscle fatigue, possibly even muscle failure.

Top-of-the-minute workouts (TOTM) provide you with 1 minute to complete the assigned sequence. Any time remaining is recovery. At the top of the next minute, you start all over again. Keep in mind that the quicker you work, the more recovery time you get, so transition between exercises quickly to maximize your workout. Chapter 9 contains instructions on performing the exercises.

Biceps curl (either suspension device or dumbbell)

suspension device row or inverted row

Rep count options are 8, 9, 10, or 12.

Note: Curls use both arms simultaneously.

Short: 4 or 5 rounds

Intermediate: 6 or 7 rounds

Long: 8 to 10 rounds

B. Switch Lunge Tabata

The goal is to create fire in your legs, primarily your quads and glutes, building explosive strength paired with endurance. The workout also provides the bonus of ankle and stability training.

Tabata, named after Japanese scientist Dr. Izumi Tabata, is 8 rounds of one or more exercises. Each round is 20 seconds in length with a rest of only 10 seconds. This workout is 8 rounds of jumping switch lunges, where your feet leave the floor as you drive up off your lead foot and switch your lead leg each rep. The first time you complete this workout you should do it without any weights. The next time you approach it, complete all 8 rounds with a set of light dumbbells in your hands. Gradually work up in weight.

You can also substitute various other exercises into any Tabata to make it more diverse, including squats, squat jumps, and push-ups. In the beginning of your training, you may even want to perform your Tabata by alternating exercises each round. Additionally, you can create other versions of Tabatas to challenge yourself and keep your body guessing, such as double Tabata (40 seconds of work, 20 seconds of rest) or various other work-to-rest ratios that also prove effective, such as a 30:15 (30 seconds of work, 15 seconds of rest).

Short: 1 Tabata (8 rounds).

Intermediate: 2 or 3 complete Tabatas (16-24 rounds total). Each Tabata remains 8 rounds, but you can take a couple minutes to rest after completing a Tabata before starting your next 8 rounds.

Long: 4 to 6 Tabatas (32-48 rounds total).

> **Note: Excessive lunges may make you extremely sore, so be careful not to overdo it.**

C. Muscle Failure Workout

The goal of this workout is to perform during oxygen debt, increase your lactic and pain thresholds, and fight off fatigue. It will also simulate the kind of fatigue you may feel in the late stages of a race.

Select a body-weight exercise and complete until failure. Recover for about 60 seconds, then complete again. If doing two separate exercises, complete each until failure, followed immediately by the next exercise. You should use separate muscle groups, so while one muscle group is depleted you can train the other. Ideally, these are bodyweight exercises, so if you have access to a suspension-device strap set, you have many more options. Here is a sample sequence:

Push-up

Squat jump

Short: 4 or 5 rounds

Intermediate: 6 or 7 rounds

Long: 8 to 10+ rounds

> **Note: This is designed for you to go until you can no longer complete reps of the given exercises. Make sure, however, that you do not sacrifice repetitions for bad form. Even if you can continue with the exercise, it is detrimental to do so if you use bad form.**

D. Burnouts

We're focused on the ability to keep working through oxygen debt and tremendous fatigue. Select one exercise and prepare to do it to failure. But this workout is different. Complete 5 reps of the exercise with a very light weight, increase the weight by 5 to 10 pounds (2.5-kg), then complete the same number of reps. Repeat until you hit muscle failure. Then work your way down backward, subtracting 5 to 10 pounds each time until you get back to your starting weight. If you're truly daring, you can attempt burnouts of the same exercise twice with a 5-minute recovery in between. Exercise options include squat, split squat, and bench press, or other exercises you choose. As with the muscle failure workout, do not sacrifice good form for higher reps. Maintain your form to the best of your ability.

Short: complete burnouts of 2 exercises

Intermediate: complete burnouts of 3 or 4 exercises

Long: complete burnouts of 5 or 6 exercises

Phase 3.1: Power and Explosiveness Workouts

By phase 3 you've reached the period of training where you have a base of strength and endurance and you have enough general fitness to begin working on power: heavier lifts, plyometrics (including weighted plyometrics), and more, typically performed with significant rest.

A. 5 × 5

The 5 × 5 refers to the number of sets and the number of reps in this workout using various exercises, such as deadlifts, squats, split squats, bench press, and weighted pull-ups—5 sets of 5 reps in this instance.

After a solid warm-up, set up your bar with a weight that challenges you to complete 5 repetitions. Remember your technique. After your 5 reps, take 2 full minutes to recover. Then repeat.

Short: 5 × 5 of 2 exercises

Intermediate: 5 × 5 of 3 exercises

Long: 5 × 5 of 4 or more exercises

B. Heavy-Carry Repeats

This workout is very similar to the heavy carries in our running workouts, but we're eliminating the running. So this workout is exclusively power, strength, and endurance. Again, you can choose the item and weight you carry. You can opt for going up and down hills repeatedly or just around a loop, but the hills will develop true power. This workout does have a massive element of endurance to it, so bear that in mind. If you want to focus more on power, opt for steep hills and heavier weight. Try some complex terrain (sand, mud, holes, gravel, etc.) once you've mastered your carries to really challenge your stability, strength, and coordination. Try for carries of 1 to 4 minutes at a time with recoveries of 1 to 2 minutes.

Short: 4 rounds

Intermediate: 6 or 7 rounds

Long: 8 to 10 rounds

C. Three-Rep Max Workout

The three-rep max is a routine you can use not just to build power but also to build a benchmark so you can gauge improvement. You will need a significant warm-up for this routine because the goal is to lift at 95 percent of your maximum for 3 repetitions. Afterward, take a 3- to 5-minute break before repeating. Lightly stretch in the interim. Potential exercises include deadlifts, squats, split squats, bench press, and weighted pull-ups. Before starting this routine, perform your standard warm-up followed by body-weight and light-weight repetitions of the exercises you plan to complete in your three-rep max.

Short: 3 rounds of each exercise

Intermediate: 5 rounds of each exercise

Long: 7+ rounds of each exercise

D. Weighted Pull-Up and Squat Jump Combination

You'll need either a weight vest for this workout or a weighted dip belt for the pull-ups and a set of dumbbells to hold for the squat jumps. The routine allows your upper body to recover while your lower body works and your lower body to recover while your upper body works. Your recovery from one exercise is your completion of the second exercise.

The most basic layout of this workout is 5 weighted pull-ups followed by 10 weighted squat jumps, although you can feel free to increase those numbers. Ideally, you want a ratio of 1 pull-up to every 2 or 3 squat jumps. There is no rest between the exercises but rather constant motion.

Short: 5 rounds

Intermediate: 10 rounds

Long: 15+ rounds

Phase 3.2: Fine-Tuning Grip Strength and Mobility Workouts

The final phase of training includes more than just power. It's about mobility, particularly in the shoulders and hips, as well as grip strength. Following are a few extra routines that should round out your training.

A. Spiderman Climber and Spiderman Push-Up Tabata

This workout is very similar to the switch lunge Tabata; we're just substituting different exercises. The goal is to engage the hips and obliques to improve your crawling abilities while also boosting strength and building endurance. Start with Spiderman climbers (chapter 7) and build to Spiderman push-ups as your strength improves. This will help you on the long crawling obstacles.

Short: 1 Tabata

Intermediate: 2 or 3 full Tabatas

Long: 4 to 6 full Tabatas

> Note: You can substitute additional exercises for the Tabatas, such as squat jumps, suspension-device exercises, and kettlebell swings, but the Spiderman climbers and Spiderman push-ups are ideal for preparing for the crawling obstacles you will encounter in your race.

B. Bear Crawl Repeats Forward and Backward

The objective of the workout is very similar to the objective of the previous one: to build strength in the core, shoulders, and legs and to develop endurance and power in the whole body to prepare you for the long crawling and challenging body-weight movements you might face in a race.

Try bear crawling (chapter 7) for a set distance, starting with 30 meters and working your way gradually up to 50 or 100 meters. Rest for 30 seconds, then crawl back. Alternatively, you can opt to jog back and repeat. For a more shoulder-intensive workout, complete some repetitions with a backward bear crawl.

Short: 5 rounds

Intermediate: 10 rounds

Long: 15+ rounds

C. Suspension-device or Pull-Up Grip Strength

For a true grip strength workout, you will need to use a pull-up bar or suspension strap. The goal is to hold on as long as possible. The suspension strap allows you to limit the pressure on your hands and grip strength, enabling you to extend the length of this workout.

If you use the pull-up bar, perform as many pull-ups as you can followed by just hanging from the bar with straight arms for an additional 30 to 60 seconds. If completing the workout on a suspension trainer, do the same workout but start with inverted rows. After you fatigue, continue to hold on for an additional 30 to 60 seconds, either with straight arms or, if you would like to make things a bit more challenging and engage your back muscles, you can complete an inverted row hold.

Short: 2 rounds

Intermediate: 3 or 4 rounds

Long: 5 or 6+ rounds

Note: If you would like to maximize grip strength on this workout, try doing pull-ups while hanging from a towel draped over the bar.

Final Thoughts

We've covered some workouts from every phase of your training, starting with foundations of strength and endurance, building up to true functional strength and lactate threshold, and finally training for speed, explosiveness, and even some fine tuning and grip strength. In chapter 11 you will see a training calendar that will help organize your training routines. You may need to refer back to this chapter as well as previous exercise chapters to finalize each daily workout's plans. If you use the materials set before you, you are on your way to a successful race.

11

Training Plans

Although a little intimidated, Chris is looking forward to taking on the right workouts to get him ready for his next obstacle race. But how should he arrange his workouts and plan his training calendar? He wants to be sure he's maximizing his training time while ensuring he's improving all aspects of OCR fitness: endurance, strength, core, mobility, power, and race-specific skills.

By now, you should have a good idea of what it takes to finish an obstacle race. We've gone over aspects of physical fitness needed for obstacle races and exercises that will help you prepare for the races. We've put everything together into actual workouts you'll complete as part of your training program. In this chapter, we provide you with an overview of your training calendar. This chapter describes the goals of each training phase along with basic guidelines for challenging yourself and taking your OCR fitness to the next level. The specific workouts listed in the training plan below can be found in Chapter 10. Be sure to refer to the specific workout in the particular training phase you're on to get the most effective experience.

Whether or not you're preparing for a 5K-length race or a longer 10+-mile (16 km+) challenge, the schedule and principles provide training advice that will prepare you for every event.

Phase 1: Foundation

Although obstacle racing tests several physical components of fitness, your main priority is to build a foundation of strength and aerobic fitness. For some, this phase may last up to 6 weeks, but 5 weeks should be enough to provide the base you'll need in order to progress to phase 2. During this phase, you'll do some running, strength, core, and muscular endurance exercises (see table 11.1), providing a foundation for the more challenging workout bouts you'll face later in the program. As much as possible, try running outdoors so your body can get acclimated to the environment on race day.

Table 11.1   Phase 1: Foundation Training Calendar

Sunday	Monday	Tuesday	Wednesday	Thursday	Friday	Saturday
Easy run 20-30 min	Easy run 25-45 min; strength workout A	Running workout A	Easy run 30-50 min; strength workout B	Running workout B	Optional active recovery	Long easy run 60-80 min
Rest day	Easy run 30-50 min; strength workout C	Running workout C	Easy run 35-55 min; strength workout D	Running workout D	Optional active recovery	Long easy run 60-90 min
Rest day	Easy run 35-55 min; strength workout A	Running workout A	Easy run 40-60 min; strength workout B	Running workout B	Optional active recovery	Long easy run 70-90 min
Rest day	Easy run 40-60 min; strength workout C	Running workout C	Easy run 45-65 min; strength workout D	Running workout D	Optional active recovery	Long easy run 70-100 min

NOTES

Workout schedule: You do not need to start your training schedule on any particular day. Make it fit your schedule. Select all workouts for these training weeks from phase 1, foundation.

Run distances: Select the length of your runs based on whether your race is short, intermediate, or long distance. Intermediate falls somewhere in the middle of the provided range; short and long are the extremes. Keep in mind that these are simply guidelines. Nothing is set in stone.

Rest and recovery: Active recovery consists of your choice of 30 to 60 minutes of cycling, swimming, or yoga. It does not mean a day of complete rest, but it will keep your muscles moving and fresh. Take advantage of these active recovery days to get your body prepared for your tough workouts on Mondays and Wednesdays. Rest days are complete rest. Just perform some light stretching and give your body a break. If you feel that 4 run days in a row are too much, break them up with recovery days in between.

Phase 2: Endurance

After building a foundation, you should be ready to take it to the next level. In phase 2, you'll focus on developing endurance and lactic threshold. This means you'll go through more rigorous training sessions (see tables 11.2 and 11.3) than you did in phase 1, which should be expected because after more than a month of foundation training you should be prepared for the next level.

Building endurance may sound straightforward enough, but what about developing lactate threshold? Simply put, lactate is a source of fuel for hard exercise and helps regulate metabolism. Lactate plays several important roles in the body, but for your training purposes, think of lactate production as a way your body produces fuel for exercise and lactic acid the by-product of working too hard. When your body can no longer produce enough lactate to support rigorous exercise, lactic acid starts to accumulate, which is accompanied by a burn in the muscles worked, typically the legs. Lactate threshold (LT) is the point where lactic acid builds up so significantly that your body fatigues and can no longer continue sustaining activity. In phase 2, one of the key goals is to develop LT, which means increasing the duration at which you can sustain vigorous activity before reaching your breaking point, or your LT. In this phase, you'll build LT with various running workouts and training circuits.

Phase 3: Power, Explosiveness, and Fine Tuning

Phase 3 is the final stage before your race. Here you'll focus on improving speed, building power, and fine-tuning skills. You'll build on strength and endurance gains from phases 1 and 2 and do functional training that obstacle athletes incorporate as part of their sport-specific training. You'll also work on grip strength and mobility in this phase. Finally, you'll master specific skills and techniques to help you overcome some of the common obstacles discussed in chapter 5.

Please note as you work through this calendar that these are general guidelines. Feel free to shape the calendar a bit more to fit your needs. Some exercises may need to be changed to make it harder or easier or a better fit for you, but the biggest key is having a plan and training with purpose through the entire process. Do your best to stay the course, to work the plan, and to remain honest with yourself, and you will find yourself improving dramatically. Finish this training plan and you will be well on your way to conquering your race.

Table 11.2 Phase 2: Endurance Training Calendar

Sunday	Monday	Tuesday	Wednesday	Thursday	Friday	Saturday
Rest day	Tempo run 20-35 min; strength workout A	Running workout A	Easy run 45-65 min; strength workout B	Running workout C	Optional active recovery	Long run 75-110 min
Rest day	Tempo run 25-40 min; strength workout C	Running workout B	Easy run 50-75 min; strength workout D	Running workout D	Optional active recovery	Long run 80-120 min
Rest day	Tempo run 30-45 min; strength workout A	Running workout A	Easy run 55-85 min; strength workout B	Running workout C	Optional active recovery	Long run 85-130 min
Rest day	Tempo run 35-50 min; strength workout C	Running workout B	Easy run 60-95 min; strength workout D	Running workout D	Optional active recovery	Long run 90-140 min

NOTES

Workout selection: Select all workouts for these 4 weeks from phase 2, endurance.

Tempo runs: Tempo runs are a much more aggressive pace, bordering on race pace. They train your body to maintain a high-quality effort despite being very uncomfortable.

Grip strength: Feel free to add grip strength and mobility work mentioned in previous exercise chapters and apply them to your active recovery days.

Table 11.3 **Phase 3: Power, Explosiveness, and Fine Tuning Training Calendar**

Sunday	Monday	Tuesday	Wednesday	Thursday	Friday	Saturday
Rest day	Easy run 35-50 min; power workout A	Running workout A	Optional active recovery; mobility workout A	Running workout B	Easy run 40-55 min; power workout D	Running workout C
Rest day	Easy run 40-60 min; power workout C	Running workout D	Optional active recovery; grip workout C	Running workout B	Easy run 45-65 min; power workout B	Running workout A
Rest day	Easy run 45-70 min; power workout A	Running workout C	Optional active recovery; mobility workout B	Running workout B	Easy run 50-75 min; power workout D	Running workout D
Rest day	Easy run 50-80 min; power workout C	Running workout A	Optional active recovery; grip workout C	Running workout B	Easy run 55-85 min; power workout B	Running workout C

NOTES
Select all workouts for these 4 weeks from phase 3.1 (power and explosiveness) or 3.2 (mobility and fine tuning).
The long run and tempo run have been eliminated because the basic runs are now fairly long and there are 3 days of speed and power running workouts. Continue to take advantage of your active recovery days, but note that mobility and grip strength work are applied to each of those days.

PART IV

PREPARING
FOR YOUR RACE

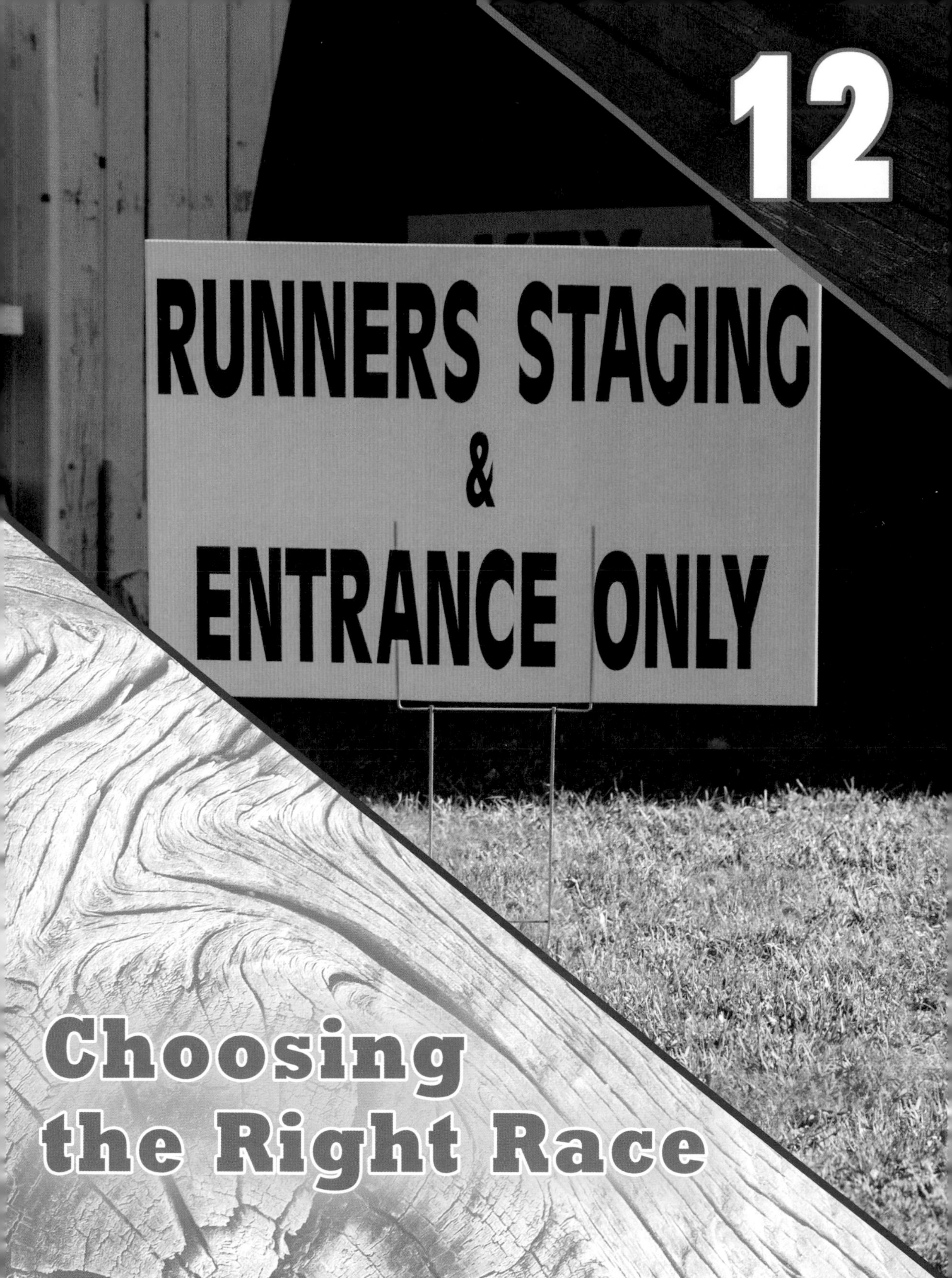
RUNNERS STAGING
&
ENTRANCE ONLY

12

Choosing the Right Race

After recalling his first obstacle racing experience, Chris thinks he may have been a little over his head in choosing the OCR he ran. How does he pick an event that will challenge him without feeling like a near-death experience? He's heard there are a variety of races for just about every fitness level, and he wants to make sure he chooses the right one for him next time.

Obstacle race organizers host hundreds, if not thousands, of events worldwide. Now scores of businesses offer an OCR for just about every fitness level and interest. You can choose from a rigorous challenge, a fun race with minimally challenging obstacles, a themed or novelty run, and many more.

With the variety of races available, how do you pick the right one for you? The right one will vary depending on several factors: your fitness level and athletic experience, goals, budget, personal preferences, and availability of races. In this chapter we review all of these considerations and touch on some of the more popular OCRs.

Fitness Level and Athletic Experience

Probably the most important factor to keep in mind when choosing a race is your fitness level. To ensure a fun, challenging race, you'll want to be sure the run is congruent with your state of fitness. Although it's not always easy to determine this because OCR organizers tend to surprise racers with unexpected obstacles, you can find the appropriate OCR for you based on your fitness level and some research.

To get a good idea of your fitness level, review the results from your fitness assessments in chapter 2. You can compare your results against the data in tables in chapter 2 to see how your starting point measures up against the fitness benchmarks listed there. This will help you determine your level of fitness. You may find that your assessment results are better for some exercises than for others, which can be expected; everyone has strengths and weaknesses. Once you've compared your results for each assessment, try to determine your average or typical performance across the board. For example, if you can do a pull-up, 8 burpees, and 15 push-ups but can hold a plank for less than 20 seconds and run 1.5 miles in 20 minutes, then you may be closer to the beginner side of the spectrum.

Even though the goal is to get to a peak level of fitness so you can crush your race, if you are a beginner or just starting with a structured exercise program, it's a good idea to start conservatively and pick an entry-level race. This will help maximize the safety and enjoyment of your first OCR. We want you coming back for more! So if you are a beginner, look for an obstacle course race of about 5 kilometers (3.1 miles), or a 5K for short. Try to schedule your race so that it's at least 3 months away. As part of your training, you can consider signing up for a traditional 5K to test and build your endurance. Once you've finished your first OCR or two, you can set your sights on a longer challenge.

If you have some exercise and running experience and performed well on the fitness assessments, you may be more of an intermediate-level athlete. You might have exercised regularly for at least a couple years or even run a road race but it's your first time taking on an obstacle course race. Or maybe it's your second time and you want to improve on your performance from your first OCR. You may be more comfortable starting with a shorter race, say 3 to 5 miles, designed for all fitness levels, possibly comparable to your first obstacle race. Try to plan your race at least 8 weeks out so you can have enough time to develop race-specific skills and improve your fitness. You can also plan a traditional road race along the way as part of your training preparation.

Goals

Your goals will dictate your OCR of choice. There are a variety of obstacle races targeting a range of goals. But most people sign up for an OCR for a few common goals: to have fun or satisfy curiosity, to challenge themselves, and to improve on performance and OCR skills.

Maybe you're curious and looking for something on the easier side that emphasizes more of the fun than competitive aspects of OCRs. Let's say you're looking for a not-too-challenging race with a minimal number of hazards associated with most events. You're just dabbling right now. If this is you, you may need to do some research. Race reviews, organizer websites, and online video walk-throughs can help you find the right one for you. In general, most 5K-length races and OCRs of similar length are designed for personal enjoyment while getting in some exercise. There are even race series held in urban areas where there is little to no mud, so you don't have to contend with unstable surfaces and slippery footwear as you try to overcome obstacles. Keep in mind that even though you can target a race that may seem safer than others, there is always some degree of risk involved. As with any sport that requires you to take on challenges, some of those challenges may play to your strengths and others may serve as motivation for improvement.

Let's say you're looking to challenge yourself. You have a race or two under your belt and you're looking to level up or improve on your performance. If your goal is the latter—to improve on a specific skill or aspect of performance—you'll want to target a race that provides you with ample opportunity to hone that skill or crush your previous personal best. You may need to do some research. So, for example, if you've been working on grip strength and climbing to conquer a horizontal (traverse) wall, rope climb or pull, or similar obstacle, you'll want to pick a race that has these obstacles. Some organizers list the obstacles on their websites. Race reviews from participants can also give you an idea of the obstacles you might find at a particular race. The extent of research you'll need to do will vary. And it may not be so in depth—you might find it's best to go back to your first or second race in which you discovered the skills you needed to improve on.

Let's say your goal is to level up: You've done a few 3- to 5-mile obstacle races, and you're ready for a new challenge. It might simply be a longer race or maybe a 6- to 8-mile event or a 3- to 5-mile race with more obstacles. For example, you might be considering a Spartan Sprint or a Tough Mudder. If this is the case, you can still use beginner-level OCRs you are familiar with as training prep for your event of choice. Familiar races can help you improve your time- and race-specific skills. You can also use longer road races as endurance prep for a longer OCR.

Maybe you want to relive your days of athletic glory. Signing up for an obstacle race means you'll want to train like an athlete not just for a single event but as a way to get in shape for your new sport. And you'll have an incredible feeling of accomplishment once you've crossed the finish line.

Maybe your goal is to be inspired. Maybe you want to race alongside others who have overcome challenges just to make it on race day. The great thing about obstacle racing is that you don't have to look far to be inspired. People sign up for obstacle races to tap in to their athletic selves and to be inspired by participants of all fitness levels around them on race day.

Are you looking for all of these challenges? No sweat. There's more than one obstacle race that will provide you with fun, challenges and plenty of inspiration. Just pick a reputable one and get out there and do it. Look for an established national or global race series or a local organizer who has a proven track record of planning and hosting obstacle races. (This way, you can address concerns of the race not taking place if the organizer goes out of business, as has been the case with some race series early on in the sport's history.)

Regardless of your goal, if it's your first or second race, you may want to think about recruiting a friend or two to join you. Racing as a team has several benefits. First, you have a support system to help you through some of the more challenging obstacles and encourage you if you feel like giving up on an especially tough race. Second, team spirit! Some teams go as far as designing T-shirts with their team names and logos to get psyched up for the race. Third, safety reasons. If you or a teammate gets hurt, you have help in calling over race staff for medical attention. Racing as part of a team can also give you some sense of accountability for your training and preparation for the race. You can exhibit team spirit even before race day. Training together will help all of your team members stay on track. You can also complete team-specific exercises to simulate the challenges you'll face as a team on race day.

Budget

Another consideration to keep in mind when choosing an obstacle race is your budget. Race fees vary across the industry. You might find a local race that charges a fee of $50 (USD) or less, while some leading organizers charge sign-up fees upwards of $200 per race. Keep an eye out for early-bird pricing because you can save by signing up ahead of time.

As you look for a race, you might notice online deals for an event you're considering. As tempting as these are, think twice before registering for an OCR through an online deals site. Hosting an obstacle race is expensive, and sometimes race organizers try an online deal to fill up race waves or because they are struggling to meet a participant quota. So, you might have to deal with either bottlenecking at obstacles or a last-minute cancellation of a race. However, this typically doesn't apply to most of the major race series, which we cover later in this chapter. Sign up through an OCR organizer's website or other reputable third-party service that is used for fulfilling registrations.

Weather and Terrain

When would you like to race? Where would you like to race? Do you want to get muddy, or do you prefer a more urban terrain? Your answers to these questions will help you narrow down your choices.

First, time of year. For some athletes, seasonality does not matter. This is especially true for those living in temperate climates or elite competitors looking to test their mettle, even in the harshest of elements. Preferences will vary among participants. Can you race in cold weather? It may not matter to you, but if you have any special health concerns, you should consider the impact of seasonality and weather conditions, including temperature (cold or hot extremes), wind, rain, and snow. You can also control the impact of weather conditions by selecting a specific race time. For example, in the summer, you can minimize the impact of heat-induced complications by signing up for an early-morning or early-evening wave.

Another consideration is terrain. Most muddy obstacle races are run on hilly terrain and off-road trails, but there are an increasing number of events organized in urban areas where mud and trails are of no concern. For the full experience of an OCR, you'll want to sign up for a muddy race. But if you're not sold on mud yet, you can try an urban or stadium race. In the long term, we recommend you at least try one obstacle course race in the great outdoors. It's how the sport started, so it's a great way to get in touch with the roots of obstacle racing and maybe even connect with nature.

You may not know exactly what you're looking for in an obstacle race until you actually do one. You can do course research, read reviews, watch participant walk-throughs, and maybe even volunteer at a race to see what the course is like from a spectator's view. All this information can help guide your decision, but until you try your first obstacle race, you might not know for sure what you'll like.

Location

Obstacle racing now has a presence in more than 30 countries. So you have many options. When searching for races, think about distance from the venue as well as training time.

Most organizers host races within 2 hours of major cities. If a race is farther than that, you can consider making a weekend vacation out of it. No car? Maybe you can find some friends to carpool with. Leading race organizers host very active online communities, so you may find a local group assembling a team to race and possibly carpool together. If you are a city dweller with no car, you may want to narrow your search to local urban races.

The race you choose may also depend on the time you have to train and prepare. If you are a beginner, give yourself at least 8 weeks to get ready for a 5K-length race.

Finding Races

There are several resources you can use to find an obstacle race. You can search the Internet using keywords such as "obstacle races" + your city or country of interest. Using the guidelines pointed out earlier, you can probably filter through search results to find a race of interest. This is the way most people found obstacle challenges not called Spartan Race, Tough Mudder, or Warrior Dash during the sport's earlier years.

The markets with the most obstacle races are the United States, Canada, UK, and Australia. Sources beyond a general Google search enable you to find an OCR just about anywhere in the world. On Active. com, you can find and sign up for hundreds of obstacle races, most held on U.S. soil. Mud and Adventure (mudandadventure.com) lists scores of mud run and obstacle racing events worldwide, with a concentration on the United States and Canada. Mud Run Guide (mudrunguide.

com) and Mud Run Fun (mudrunfun.com) also list obstacle events in the United States and Canada.

Several resources track and list obstacle races outside of the United States. Muddy Race (www.muddyrace.co.uk) contains a directory and event listing of obstacle races held in the UK. Obstacle Racers Australia (www.obstacleracers.com.au) lists more than 40 organizers holding OCRs in Australia. OCR Europe (www.ocreurope.com) contains a comprehensive calendar of events in Europe.

Even though you can fall back on these sites for an OCR near you, there are some leading companies worth mentioning. The following race profiles should guide you in your search for a race that's right for you.

Major Race Organizations

In a few years, obstacle racing rapidly spread across the globe. Although there isn't sufficient data to determine just how many organizers there are, it's safe to say that you can probably find an obstacle race held within two hours of most major cities.

Spartan Race

Spartan Race holds obstacle races worldwide and for a variety of fitness levels. For the advanced athletes, the Spartan Beast is a 12+-mile (19+ km) course with more than 20 obstacles. The Spartan Super is best for intermediate-advanced level exercisers because it covers roughly 8 to 10 miles (12-16 km) and more than 15 obstacles. Although these two may sound intense, there is also a version for newbies.

The Spartan Sprint, 3 to 5 miles (5-8 km) in length, is positioned for beginners and others new to obstacle racing. Even though it's one of their shorter races, it's not an easy race. As a stepping-stone to a Spartan Sprint in the great outdoors, you can try a Spartan Sprint in select major league ballparks across the United States. These can be just as challenging as Spartan Sprints held on trails but scaled back to around 2 to 3 miles.

Tough Mudder

Tough Mudder is a 10- to 12-mile (16+ km) challenge with at least 20 obstacles. Intuitively, you would expect the Tough Mudder to attract advanced athletes, but first-time obstacle participants also sign up for the challenge. It's not uncommon for beginners to sign up as part of a team to have some accountability with training and racing. Tough Mudder is held in the United States, UK, Canada, and Australia as well as other international locations, all of which are listed on their website, https://toughmudder.com.

Warrior Dash

The Warrior Dash is a 5K (3.1-mile) obstacle race with approximately 12 obstacles. Warrior Dash has held events in the United States, Australia, New Zealand, Europe, and Mexico. While Spartan Race and Tough Mudder emphasize the challenging aspects of an obstacle race, Warrior Dash positions their series as a fun, doable run for all fitness levels. However, Warrior Dash also holds competitive waves for those striving to qualify for their annual championships. Event listings are available on Warrior Dash's website, www.warriordash.com.

Final Thoughts

By now, you should have a good idea of how you'll go about choosing a race that's right for you. There's at least one event that you'll enjoy and will make you want to go back for more. Keep in mind your fitness level, athletic experience, goals, budget, and preferences as you do your research. And give yourself enough time to prepare so you can crush your first (or next) obstacle race.

13

Injury Prevention and Management

Throughout his first race, Chris noticed several racers stop well before the finish line for several reasons. Someone sprained an ankle after a bad fall, a couple people didn't look where they were going and stray branches cut them, and one person hurt a shoulder while attempting the monkey bars. Chris felt lucky to finish the race with only a few minor cuts and bruises, but he has a feeling he can't rely on luck next time. What can he do to prevent injuries on race day?

If you've heard of obstacle racing, chances are you've come across a news story reporting the dangers of the sport. Cuts, bumps, bruises, and more serious skeletal injuries and complications such as bacterial infections can make obstacle racing a hazardous endeavor. The good news is that you can prevent most of these injuries. But be aware that, as with all sports, injury risks are a part of obstacle racing. Beyond trusting your common sense and listening to your body on race day, you can take measures to prevent injuries. In this chapter, we cover some of the common injuries in obstacle racing and training, how to prevent them, and how to manage them if they happen to you.

With the challenges you'll face in training and racing, you can expect exposure to a range of injuries and complications. Common injuries can affect skin, muscles, bones, and joints. You can't prevent everything, but you can prevent and manage some situations as you train and race.

Many injuries and complications affecting the muscles, bones, and joints, can be attributed to overtraining and/or over-racing. Sometimes your best prevention is simply paying attention to your body. If you are feeling sore longer than usual after your workouts or racing events, getting frequent colds or other infections, lacking motivation to train, depressed, irritable, or having trouble sleeping, you may be overtraining. In this case, scale back and consider skipping any upcoming races you have in your calendar so that your body and mind can take an extended break to repair and recover. Sometimes all you need is a week or two of less intense training with a focus on moderate aerobic exercise, flexibility work, and maybe even a sports massage.

In addition to overtraining, another common cause of many muscle and bone issues is poor form with running and exercise moves. Using proper form with training exercises should be straightforward enough: be sure to follow our instructions with each move covered in chapters 6-11. When running, be sure to stand up tall, but keep your shoulders relaxed. When your foot hits the ground for each stride during endurance running, which is what you'll primarily work on in this program, make sure it lands directly under your body. If you feel any lingering soreness and pain in your shoulders or lower body muscles and joints after your running sessions, consider getting a gait analysis from your local running store or club to troubleshoot and correct your form.

We'll get into depth into the common issues affecting the muscles, bones, and joints later on in the chapter. First, we'll start with your body's first line of protection against the elements of an obstacle race: your skin.

Skin Irritations

Like any outdoor activity, obstacle racing can pit you against nature's elements, placing you at risk of bug bites, rashes, and other skin irritations. Keep this in mind, especially if you are preparing for a typical obstacle race that will take you through trails and woods. On race day, use bug-repellant lotion, spray, or wipes to protect your skin. An additional layer of thin, breathable compression wear can help protect you against irritations caused by brushing up against poison ivy and stray branches. (See chapter 3 for more on race-day apparel.) Plan to wash up soon after the event to remove any irritants; you can use a poison ivy wash such as Tecnu to remove the oils from your skin if you know you are susceptible to ivy rashes. If you are extremely allergic to pollen, you might want to check with your doctor for the appropriate allergy medication to take on race day.

Cuts and Lacerations

Simple cuts and lacerations may be the most common injuries, particularly among obstacle newbies. Running too close to a stray branch, crawling under barbed wire or over rocks, and negotiating similar hazards of the course can put you at risk for cuts and scratches. Wearing fitted tops and bottoms can help reduce the risk, but in the event you do get a cut or laceration, be sure to take the proper precautions.

If it's a simple surface cut that doesn't break the skin, you can probably continue with your race without medical attention. But be mindful of deeper cuts and lacerations. Try not to let the wound get in contact with dirty water for too long. If there's a rest stop or first-aid area along the way, rinse it out and get a waterproof bandage. If a simple rinse and bandage won't stop the bleeding, look for staff who will help you get medical attention as soon as possible.

Windburn

If you live in a warm climate, you might not have to worry about windburn. But if you live in a colder region and have a race planned in the fall or winter seasons, you should make the proper preparations. First, make sure you've applied enough moisturizer to your skin, especially parts exposed to the environment such as your face, ears, and hands. Consider facewear designed for athletes, which is often made up of material that wicks away moisture and allows for breathability while protecting your face from the wind.

It's not just your face that can be susceptible to wind. In cold, windy weather, the rest of your body needs an additional layer of protection. Gloves for your hands and thermal compression wear for your torso, arms, and lower body can help keep you warm and protect you from windburn. Layering also helps.

Sunburn

You may not have to worry about windburn if you live in a warm climate or during the milder months of the year, but with any prolonged time spent outdoors, you run the risk of a sunburn or worse. Be sure to protect your skin against the sun and other rays with a waterproof sunscreen. If you are in for a longer race, try to take a small tube of sunscreen with you to reapply throughout the event. To protect the surface of your head from the sun, you can also consider wearing a bandana, cap, or sports hat of some sort. Otherwise, if you are bald and choose not to equip with headwear, be sure to apply sunscreen to your head and reapply throughout the race.

Chafing

As with any running activity, chafed skin can happen in obstacle racing. Inner thighs, heels, and feet tend to be most prone to chafing. The best strategy for chafing is prevention. Compression shorts can help keep your inner thighs from rubbing, helping reduce the likelihood of chafing. You can prevent chafed heels by wearing properly fitted footwear. Your running and training shoes should fit snugly, not slip, on your heels, to avoid chafing around the heels. You can also apply lotion, Vaseline, or roll-on gels that prevent chafing.

Foot Blisters, Corns, and Calluses

Probably more than any other body part, your feet take a beating from training and racing. Long-duration runs, jumping, and traversing over unsteady terrain take a toll on your feet. Some of the most common foot ailments runners face are blisters and calluses.

If you've gone on a long run, you're familiar with foot blisters, which are usually caused by excessive rubbing of the skin against shoes or socks. Footwear slippage can also cause blisters. Sometimes excessive rubbing and footwear slippage can be further complicated by worn-down footwear or improperly fitted shoes. Ill-fitting shoes and wet, uncomfortable socks are common culprits of blisters. So, for starters, make sure you have properly fitted footwear and comfortable athletic socks. As a general rule, replace running and training shoes every 300 to 500 miles (480-800 km); this simple practice will help prevent other foot- and muscle injuries during training.

If you are serious about getting into longer obstacle runs and have found yourself prone to blisters, you may want to consider getting a gait analysis. Your body may be making some compensations, causing your feet to rub against socks and shoes excessively. Most running centers and some retail outlets that sell running shoes offer a gait analysis and can help you identify compensations and corrective exercises. This can ensure you are running efficiently and effectively so as to reduce your risk for blistering or worse damage to your feet.

Sometimes even with the best prevention efforts, you find yourself with a blister after a long run or particularly challenging obstacle trek. Try to avoid the temptation of popping the blister; you may risk an infection and need a longer recovery time as a result. If you have a blister, let your feet air out. Wear sandals or other open-toed shoes when possible. Keep the blister and surrounding area clean. These simple steps might help treat it in no time. However, for stubborn blisters, consider seeing your primary care physician or a podiatrist to treat it. If you do pop a blister, make sure to do it only after you've cleaned it along with the surrounding area and be sure to have antibiotic ointment or gel and gauze handy to place over the blister. Do not remove the skin covering the blister once you've popped it, because removing the skin can increase the chances of infection.

Calluses are another common complication that can affect the skin on your feet. These are a result of the build-up of hard skin, usually around the heel or sole of the foot. Again, proper footwear can help prevent calluses, as will good jumping, walking, and running mechanics. If you are new to high-impact training, you may need some cushioning in your training shoes at the start. Sometimes, though, calluses are the by-product of the wear and tear common in athletic training. One simple home treatment is to soak your feet in water and use a pumice stone to gently break down the hardened skin. Pharmacies also sell over-the-counter creams to help treat calluses.

Muscles and Fascia

Training and racing hard can put you at high risk for injuring or simply tweaking muscles. Because obstacle racing challenges your body head to toe, it's important to be aware of the common injuries that affect muscles, fascia, and tendons.

Plantar Fasciitis

Although more common in older people, plantar fasciitis can also affect athletes who spend a lot of time on their feet, including obstacle racers. Plantar fasciitis is the inflammation of connective tissue that connects the heel bone to the toes. If you have plantar fasciitis, the sole of your foot will feel painful and extremely tight, particularly when you stand, walk, or try to run. As you can imagine, it's very difficult to train on your feet with this condition.

The good news is that you can help prevent plantar fasciitis. Sometimes, making sure you have the right shoes will address this and many other foot and lower-leg issues. Often plantar fasciitis is associated with tight and weak calf muscles. Before any workout that involves a lot of running and jumping, warm up the muscles supporting your lower leg and feet. Calf stretches and raises can help prepare your lower legs and feet for activity. Walking around barefoot, particularly outdoors on grass or blunt pebbles, will help stretch out and warm up the soles of your feet. Stretching devices designed to improve flexibility around the lower leg and plantar fascia can also help with prevention measures.

You can also roll out your plantar fascia as you would for fascia surrounding your other muscle groups. Some athletes use tennis, golf, or lacrosse balls to roll out the soles. Which one you use will depend on the severity of the tightness on the soles and your pain threshold. If the plantar fascia are extremely tight, you may want to start with a tennis ball and work up to lacrosse and golf balls.

If you start to feel swelling on the soles of your feet, some rest, mild stretching, and rolling might be enough to alleviate the pain. You can also try icing your foot—a half-liter bottle with frozen water can comfortably fit underfoot. If pain worsens and persists after a few weeks, consider seeing your primary doctor or a podiatrist.

Calf and Achilles Injuries

Working our way up from the feet, the next common setback for runners affects the Achilles and calves. Although Achilles and calf complications each have distinct symptoms, the causes are often similar: insufficient warm-up and poor flexibility. Those with tight and weak muscles are at a high risk of suffering from calf and Achilles problems. You can use a foam roll to alleviate tightness and do some dynamic flexibility exercises such as lunges and single-leg work to warm up your lower legs for activity, all of which can decrease the likelihood of injuring your Achilles and calves. A common stretch is a heel drop while standing on a step (see figure 13.1). Ensure you have enough spring in your training shoes so that there is a balance of support and flexibility for your lower-leg muscles and tendons to move with ease. Restrictive footwear can worsen Achilles tendinitis and other problems.

FIGURE 13.1　Proper Achilles warm-up.

But even with the best prevention efforts, sometimes something has to give when you push your body to the limits. And with all the running, jumping, and speed work you'll do to prepare for race day, your Achilles tendon will get a lot of work as the structure that connects your calf muscles to your heel bone. If the tendon is placed under excessive stress, it can tear or rupture, which is a worst-case scenario that can take several months to recover from. Before that happens, though, there are some warning signs. Some pain or inflammation along the Achilles may signal that you should get some rest or scale back your training. Swimming and cycling to maintain cardiorespiratory fitness are good alternatives to running as your Achilles recovers. You can also take some time to address any weak lower-leg muscles or imbalances in the calf and muscles supporting your shins, including the tibialis and peroneal muscles. Don't take Achilles pain lightly because ignoring it can set your training back more than anticipated. If you feel persistent pain, see your doctor.

For calves, complications and injuries can vary. As with most training that involves your feet, it won't be uncommon for you to feel some general calf soreness. This usually means you need to spend some time before and after your workout warming up and cooling down with calf stretches. Often this will help alleviate soreness. Soreness is a sign that your body is responding and adapting to the new rigors of training. Once your body adapts as you continue to engage in flexibility exercises for the calves, soreness should decrease over time. Again, make sure you have properly fitted shoes that provide adequate cushioning. And remember to replace running and training shoes every 300 to 500 miles (480-800 km).

Beyond general soreness, you should be aware of three types of calf strains along with corresponding management and treatment methods:

Grade 1

DEFINITION   Overstretching of the calf muscles that might have caused slight tearing.

TREATMENT   Rest and some light activity with flexibility and foam rolling. Exercising in the pool and swimming to maintain aerobic fitness are also options. Listen to your body and pain threshold because the time it takes for a grade 1 sprain to fully heal varies from a couple weeks to a month or two. Don't hesitate to get help from a doctor, especially if pain continues after a few weeks.

Grade 2

DEFINITION   Partial tearing of muscle fibers.

TREATMENT   Rest and physical rehabilitation. At this point, if you feel a lot of pain in your calves, you don't want to troubleshoot your injury alone. Get help because grade 2 strains and worse call for the expertise of a doctor and possibly a physical therapist. With good treatment, you may recover from a grade 2 sprain in 6 to 8 weeks.

Grade 3

DEFINITION   Complete tearing or rupturing of muscle fibers.

TREATMENT   Extensive rehab and possible surgery. Grade 3 strains often require a complete break from activity, which would include working out and, of course, obstacle racing.

Hamstring Problems

Hamstring problems and injuries may be even more common among runners, obstacle racers, and similar athletes than calf complications. And if you spend most of your daytime at a desk, you can be at an increased risk of injuring your hamstrings because they are continually shortened throughout the day. Most hamstring problems arise from tight or weak hamstrings, muscle imbalances, and overuse from activities such as running. The good news is that you can prevent hamstring problems.

As with many other injuries, prevention measures start with your exercise program. This program will help you ensure hamstring flexibility and strength and address muscular imbalances. Most people have stronger quadriceps muscles (muscles of the front thigh above the knee) and weaker hamstring muscles, which support the back of the thigh above the knee. This imbalance can put you at risk for developing hamstring injuries, so strength exercises targeting the hamstrings will help you restore balance. Warming up is a must because it will prepare your hamstrings for activity, and it's during your warm-up and cool-down that you'll do most dynamic and static flexibility exercises.

But even with the best prevention efforts, elite athletes can succumb to hamstring injuries and setbacks. Sometimes it's just slight pain or soreness, which can be addressed with rest, ice, and massage. Sometimes it's more serious. Like calves, hamstrings can suffer from a range of strains with various degrees of treatment. If pain continues even once you've rested and applied ice, visit your doctor so you can manage, treat, and recover from the injury.

Adductor and Hip Problems

As you've noticed, obstacle racing requires a lot of work and movement from the lower body, which places you at risk for overworking and possibly injuring just about any muscle in your legs. The adductors and hips are no exception. Like many other leg injuries, overuse, tightness, and muscular imbalances can lead to setbacks. So can bad form with exercises.

Your training program, starting with the warm-up will help you prevent problems in the adductors and hips. Raise your core temperature with light activity and do some dynamic flexibility exercises such as leg swings and hip rotations to prepare the adductors and hips for activity. Adjusting workload cautiously will help. Gradually increase your running distance and volume of strength work. The 10 percent principle applies here: Try not increase your total distance or volume by more than 10 percent a week.

If pain in your adductors and hips continues, you know the drill. Contact your physician and get treatment from a specialist. During this time, training in the pool may be a way to continue working on your obstacle fitness in a low-impact environment.

Iliotibial Band Pain

The hips, and the knees to an extent, are prone to tightness and weakness in connection with the iliotibial (IT) band, the tendon that extends from your hip bone to the outside of your tibia, a lower-leg bone. When you bend your knee, the IT band bends and slides over the outside of the knob of your knee (femur). So whether you are running, cycling, doing a lot of squats, or simply sitting down for too long, your IT bands deal with a lot of stress. When the IT band is tight, you may feel tightness and maybe even some pain along the outside of the knee, hip, and even glutes. Flexibility exercises as well as foam rolling will help loosen the IT band and prevent pain. You can do a foam roll as part of your warm-up after doing some light calisthenics and body-weight work to raise your core temperature.

Tight IT bands can put you at risk for IT band syndrome, which will feel like persistent, significant pain outside of the knee. IT band pain and syndrome can affect novice and veteran runners as well as obstacle athletes. Stretching and foam rolling will help, but so will properly fitted running and training shoes. If your shoes are worn out, your body will end up absorbing a lot of the impact, placing your joints and tendons, including the IT bands, at risk for injury. If you run on a track or loop, remember to change direction regularly so you're not stressing the knees at the same angle every time.

Some knee pain attributable to IT band tightness can be addressed with rest, ice, and foam rolling. However, if knee pain persists for more than a week, see a doctor. In the meantime, you may be able to engage in low-impact activities like swimming, rowing, and possibly cycling, depending on your pain threshold and the extent of IT band injury.

Back Pain and Injuries

All the running, jumping, and other high-impact activity associated with training and racing can take a cumulative toll on your back, especially if it's not prepared. Weak core musculature, which supports your back, is often associated with low back pain, regardless of your activity level. So if you do too much too fast in your training without building the proper foundation, then you are at a higher risk of hurting your back. Poor posture and flexibility can also contribute to back-related injuries. If you sit a lot for work, get up regularly, walk around, and maybe even do a few stretches.

Fortunately, this exercise program includes core and mobility training to strengthen the muscles supporting your back and increase total-body flexibility. Several of the exercises introduced earlier increase core strength: plank, bird dog, Superman, mountain climber, ab rollout, and even the push-up. Those chapters also detail exercises that improve the mobility of muscles supporting the back: glute and piriformis stretches, child's pose, foam rolling, leg swings, and multiplanar lunges. Although many of these exercises build the foundation of your training program in phase 1, you will continue to incorporate them during the course of your training to maintain core strength, flexibility, and mobility.

If you find yourself suffering from low back pain anytime during any part of your training program, sometimes rest and ice for a few days are enough for recovery. While you're sidelined, you can take some of your training to the pool to maintain fitness or focus on recovery workouts and mind–body exercises such as yoga. If back pain persists, see your doctor.

Shoulder Problems

Strength and power exercises involving the shoulder as well as obstacles like monkey bars and some climbs can all pose a potential injury risk to this muscle group. Some of the more common shoulder injuries that affect obstacle athletes are strains (grades 1, 2, and 3) and rotator cuff tears. Strains follow a similar progression as discussed earlier (in the Calf and Achilles Injuries section). A rotator cuff tear is a tearing of one or more of the small stabilizer muscles of the shoulder. Rotator cuff tears are often associated with nagging or acute pain deep inside the front shoulder. In addition to strains and rotator cuff injuries, prolonged soreness and tightness after training sessions involving lifts with heavy weight are common shoulder issues. The good news is that you can take measures to prevent injuries and setbacks.

Often, bad form and use of weights that are too heavy for you when performing maximal strength exercises can lead to shoulder injury. Monkey bars and climbs done with poor technique or attempted when your shoulders are not strong enough can also contribute to injury. A sound exercise program with progressive strength training and flexibility work, as this one incorporates, will help prevent these complications.

Follow instructions on proper form for shoulder exercises and challenges that involve this muscle. Sometimes it's a good idea to try a few reps of a strength or power exercise involving the shoulder exercise using light weight so your body can get used to the move and as a warm-up before going full out. As you get stronger, monitor weight increases for lifts and shoulder exercises, particularly overhead lifts and shoulder presses. Make note of any pain or discomfort. And adhere to the 10 percent rule.

Shoulder injuries should not be taken lightly. Any shoulder pain, injury, or muscle tweak not addressed puts you at risk for further injury. Continuing to train with shoulder problems typically means your body will start to compensate by overrecruiting muscles in your neck and back to execute challenging exercises, which can lead to injuries in those muscle groups as well. If you feel any shoulder pain or discomfort, rest and ice until it heals or at least scale back on exercises that engage the shoulder for your next several workouts. Don't underestimate or overlook some exercises that engage the shoulder such as planks, push-ups, and even seal walks. Listen to your body as your shoulder improves and gradually work your way up to adjusting the load to make exercises more challenging while monitoring your shoulder's response. If all else fails or if pain continues, see your doctor or other medical specialist.

Skeletal Problems

Now that you have a good idea of the injury risks associated with muscles and surrounding connective tissue when training and obstacle racing, let's move on to the ligaments, bones, and joints. Injuries to the skeletal system often take longer to recover from than injuries to muscles, so it's important to be aware of the risks and how to prevent them. Unlike injuries affecting the skin and muscle, it's not recommended to try to treat skeletal injuries with home remedies alone because you typically need help from a physician for these setbacks.

Ankle Sprains

Ankle sprains are among the most common injuries on the OCR course for beginners. Maybe it's no surprise: You can turn an ankle on unstable terrain from jumping with bad landing mechanics or simply because you didn't train appropriately for your first challenge. Even before race day, ankle sprains are not uncommon during training because running and plyometrics require ankle elasticity and strength in muscles surrounding the ankles. And if they're not ready for high-impact work, the risk of ankle injury is further elevated.

As with muscle strains, there are a few degrees of ankle sprains. If you think your ankle has taken a bad turn, check with your doctor if you are unsure of the severity.

Grade 1

DEFINITION Slight tearing and damage to ligament fibers; little to no swelling or pain.

TREATMENT Rest and ice are often enough, but the extent of rest varies. For some, several days may be enough, while others may need a couple weeks. Scale back on jumps and running workouts. Listen to your body with any exercise.

Grade 2

DEFINITION Partial tearing and other damage to ligament fibers; some swelling and pain.

TREATMENT More rest, maybe even several weeks' worth. During this time, you may need to focus on training that excludes any use of the ankle and focus leg and lower-body training on simple stretching and strengthening exercises for muscles surrounding the ankle, such as single-leg work. Physical therapy is a likely option in this case for a safe and speedy recovery. You will probably need to cancel any races in the weeks after a grade 2 sprain until you fully recover.

Grade 3

DEFINITION Complete tearing of the ligament fibers; significant swelling and pain.

TREATMENT Even more rest, ranging from 3 to 6 months. At this point, you'll likely need to lay off any physical activity that involves your feet. Physical therapy is a must because you might not even be able to walk. Surgery is also a possibility if the ankle does not improve after a couple months with physical therapy and rest from high-impact activity.

Shin Splints

Shin splints overlap with muscular problems because they primarily affect the muscle groups and tendons in the lower leg, which surround and support the shin. Shin splints are overstressed muscles at the front of the lower leg, which result in severe pain in the shin area. This injury is often caused by overuse and pounding, which are common with running or jumping. To prevent, be aware of how much pounding your feet do during a run or a jumping exercise. It takes time and a lot of conscious effort to correct, but the lighter you can be on your feet, the less likely you'll suffer from shin splints.

If you have some pain in the shins, sometimes walking on your heels as much as you can will help you recover faster because it will reduce the impact your shins typically absorb as you step with your normal gait. Even walking on your heels for just 5 to 10 minutes per day can help as your shins recover. If you have more severe pain, substitute biking or swimming for your running workouts while you recover.

Stress Fractures

Most common in the feet and legs, stress fractures are often due to overuse and repetitive weight-bearing activity. Runners, basketball players, tennis players, and now obstacle athletes need to be aware of it. Again, the best way to prevent stress fractures is through your training programs. Try not to do too much too early. Gradually progress the work volume, load, and intensity of your workouts so that your body has time to adapt.

Sometimes it's hard to detect stress fractures without the help of an x-ray. But if you feel persistent pain in the lower legs or even your upper body for a prolonged time, maybe even months, and can't attribute it to any of the other injuries discussed here, a stress fracture may be a possibility. See your doctor for a diagnosis. Stress fractures can take months of recovery and often require complete rest or reduced activity, especially those having to do with maximal effort.

Actual Breaks

Actual broken bones are not as common as many may have been led to believe with obstacle racing. However, they are possible, especially with those who haven't trained adequately or trained too hard too early. Detecting an actual break isn't much of a mystery—your body will be the first to tell you. Sometimes you can even hear it happen, followed by severe pain. Get help: See your doctor, physical therapist, or other specialist and get plenty of rest for the affected bones.

Final Thoughts

By now, you should have a good grasp of the common injuries linked to obstacle racing. You can prevent many of them through the training program outlined in this book and by listening to your body and using common sense on race day. If you get sidelined from injury, you can take measures toward a full recovery. Above all, if you are uncertain about the extent of an injury, see your doctor and get help with treatment. The last thing you want is for an injury to keep you from the mud any longer than necessary.

14

Mental
Training
and Preparation

Chris is 45 minutes into his race when he rolls his ankle and falls while descending a steep hill. It's swelling up and causing him a great deal of difficulty on descents. To make matters worse, he damaged his hydration pack in the fall and it's no longer functioning. Chris planned to rely on the pack to keep hydrated throughout the long race and he's now moving at a pace significantly slower than expected. He's fallen behind his friends and is now trudging along alone. It's times like these that mental strength comes in handy, and Chris will need to tap into every bit of it to conquer what remains of the course and reach his goals. He's about to find out how tough and determined he is. And for many, this is the point of racing in the first place.

Strength and speed are important, but if you lack toughness, you'll struggle to succeed. You can prepare for the physical rigors of a race all you want, but if you don't prepare your mind, you're setting yourself up for failure. It's not necessarily the strongest athlete who prevails, conquers, and reaches goals; it is the mentally strong athlete.

Value of Mental Training

Mental toughness can be a complete game changer for your race. It can help you persevere and carry on during what can sometimes become dark moments during your race. It can help you get the most out of your race experience. But you must train your mind to handle the stresses not just of your race but of your training as well. Doing so will reap benefits for your race because you'll be prepared when race day comes. It will allow you to train longer, harder, and with more consistency.

Training for your race can become a grind. There are days you'll be tremendously excited to get out there and put in a workout. There will be other days that you have no desire to put in the effort. On some days you will feel too sore to train. And there will be days that you get partway through the workout and feel exhausted. It's your mental strength that will carry you through those workouts. That mental toughness will then carry over on race day. And when you get to race day, you'll be ready to perform at your highest level. On race day, you won't crack under fatigue. You won't buckle from the pain. And you will run your best possible race because you will be mentally unbreakable. During your training and races, you can employ several methods to make yourself mentally stronger, such as using visualization and breathing techniques, repeating mantras, and harnessing your emotions.

Visualization and Breathing Techniques

Visualization prepares the mind for training and for races to come. Visualization can be applied during your workouts, before your races, and during the event itself.

During workouts, visualization can get you through the tough days. Finding a way to zone out and just keep your feet moving can be a huge help during long runs, especially if you're not feeling well or not enjoying it. Visualization allows you to send your mind to another place. You can essentially space out. Focus on your breathing and envision your race. Get lost in the idea of your event. Imagine the obstacles, the up hills and down hills, the people you'll be running with, and the thrill of the finish. Find your intrinsic motivation and focus on it.

Visualization the night before your event can take your performance on race day to a higher level. Combined with breathing techniques, this is one of the best ways to calm your mind and keep you focused on succeeding.

Sometimes the night before a race, doubt can start to creep in. Fear, anxiety, and hesitation can all become factors that negatively affect your race. Instead, focus on all of the great things you've done with your training. Appropriate breathing goes hand in hand with your visualization. Lie back, place your hands across your abdomen, and breathe deeply. What you're looking for is diaphragmatic breathing. You'll know you're doing it correctly if your abdomen goes up and down, which you can feel with your hands placed on your midsection.

Close your eyes, breathe deeply for 5 minutes, and envision your race. Think about your preparations, your training, and your fueling. Imagine the starting line, the obstacles, and the finish. Keep your thoughts relaxed and positive. Diaphragmatic breathing should be employed not just the night before the race but also every night of your training.

When race day arrives, you may need to employ visualization again. You might struggle at times during the race. Fatigue and a bit of pain can bring on feelings of doubt. You'll need to mentally go to that place you went to during your workouts, envisioning the positive things about the race and all the hard work you've put in. Control your breathing, slow your mind and just focus on your tasks, one at a time.

Picturing success can be key as well. Basketball coaches often tell their players to visualize the ball going through the basket as they shoot it because it allows the mind to hone in on a specific goal and improve accuracy. The same concepts can be applied to your race. At the bottom of every hill, visualize yourself climbing over the summit. Any time you have a moment of doubt, visualize that finish. Imagine the pictures you'll be taking with your friends, that medal around your neck, or maybe the cold beers or waters in your hand at the finish line. Picture the stories you'll be telling your coworkers about your conquest on Monday morning once you get there. Find your reason to finish strong and use it to fuel you.

Similarly, there are visualization techniques during the race that can keep you moving forward strong through the tough times. As you run up a hill, imagine you've got a magnet connected to your waist and it's pulling your right to the top. If people are passing you, use that to your advantage. I use the expression all the time, "make them your mule." Envision that person running by as doing the work for you. Latch onto them, trying to shadow their every step, drafting off them, knowing that they are making your life easier by helping you set a pace and cutting through the wind for you. Imagine they are your mule and they are doing the work for you.

Once you master visualization, you'll reach another plane during your race where time will float by, the difficult challenges will be a breeze and you will find a new level of enjoyment with the experience.

Repeating Mantras

Mantras are an effective way to stay positive and motivated both in training and on race day. A mantra is a word, phrase, or sound that aids in concentration and focus, generally used in meditation. Elite athletes have been incorporating it in their training and competitions for years. A mantra can allow you to keep your mind focused on the task at hand.

Here are examples of mantras that you can repeat to yourself:

➤ Quitting is not an option!
➤ One foot in front of the other!
➤ Just one more ____!
➤ Nothing else matters!

Whether you choose one of these mantras or find your own, the key is to adopt that mantra and absorb it into your life. Repeat it to yourself during workouts and in the difficult portions of your races. Find strength in it. It can be your security blanket when things get tough during your race.

Harnessing Your Emotions

The harnessing of emotions is probably the most difficult part of preparation for mental toughness because it's such a subjective concept. You'll become better at it as your training progresses, but the most important key is to keep your thoughts residing in the positive. Never let negative emotions control you.

Feelings like doubt, self-pity, and anger can rapidly seize control of your thoughts in a race, especially when you're dehydrated, exhausted, or even slightly hurt. You'll need to learn to avoid those thoughts at all costs. You know ahead of time that those are thoughts that might cross your mind. Have a plan to ignore them before they ever start. Having a planned response to any of those particular thoughts can help.

Here are some examples:

This is stupid. I've been at this for hours and I'm still miles from the finish. Why even bother?

You've been training for months. Did you expect it to be easy? The more difficult it is, the more worth it that finish will be and the more accomplished you will feel.

My legs hurt and I'm tired. I'm over this.

You knew what you were getting yourself into beforehand. This is what you came for. It's the challenge.

I can't go on. I can't do it.

Yes. You can. Just keep moving. Just keep smiling.

This isn't fun anymore.

Nobody ever said the whole race would be fun. See the fun in it. And you'll have mostly fond memories of it once it's over.

Making Misery Your Ally

Obstacle racing isn't just about purely enjoying yourself. Sure, you'll have moments of absolute joy, of fun, of triumph. But you'll also have plenty of moments of outright misery. You may experience anger, frustration, or even despair. So you need to go into your race expecting that. After all, those feelings are what make your triumph, your victory so special. Without them, it's just a race you finished.

You'll want to be prepared for the things that will bring on those negative feelings. The best way to do so is to grow mentally stronger by training your weaknesses. We all love to train our strengths. Runners love to go for a run. Strong folks love to lift weights. But truly taking the next step with your training and your mentality will require you to train your weaknesses. Focus on the things you aren't good at, add them to your routine day after day until you make those things strengths. Repeat them so much in training that when you get to those moments in your race, you feel nothing but your comfort zone.

For many, it will simply be running big hills. For others, it's the heavy carries that bring on that feeling of despair. Fifteen minutes into a heavy carry, when your fingers, back and shoulders are giving out, you want to be able to think to yourself, "I've done this a thousand times. This time is no different."

Once you've reached that point, mentally, you'll know you'll be a tough person to stop. And that's the point. Making yourself unstoppable, or at least believing so. Your mind will carry your body far beyond your physical breaking point if you just prepare it to do so and accept that's the expectation. Make misery your ally and you will conquer your race.

Final Thoughts

Whatever you need to tell yourself to keep on moving and working, just keep doing that. In the end, you will be so grateful you did. Continue to think positive thoughts, keep your head up and your negative emotions in check, and you will succeed. And that's a philosophy that isn't just valuable for race day. It's valuable for life.

15

Countdown to Race Day

With a sound exercise program in hand, Chris is now ready to prepare for his next obstacle race. Training won't be easy, but a challenging sports-specific plan like the one he will complete in this book will be just what he needs to have the confidence and readiness to endure the race. Beyond training prep, there are a few logistical items Chris needs to keep in mind looking ahead to the event.

Congratulations on getting this far! If you've completed the training programs outlined in this book, you can be confident that you're ready for your obstacle race. You've worked on strength, endurance, power, core strength, agility, and mental fitness for obstacle racing. Now for the best part: the race.

In this chapter, we provide you some tips to help you prepare for race day. We also provide guidelines on racing etiquette for the course. The week or two leading up to your race is an ideal time to work on any final preparations you need for your race. Let's start with a couple weeks out from your race and work up to the actual day.

Two Weeks Before the Race

At least a couple weeks before the event, you should start gathering some of the items you'll need for the race. If you have a race or two under your belt, you might not need to plan this far ahead. But if it's your first race, by this time, you should think about things you need for game day. Figure 15.1 lists essential race-day items.

Go through a checklist of these items at least two weeks before the race in case you don't have some of these essentials at home. That way, you'll have some time to pick them up or order online. Once you have the things you'll need, you won't have to think about them and can focus on getting your body ready for the race.

One Week Before the Race

The week before your race is typically time to scale back on your training to ensure your body has enough time to recover and be ready for the challenges you'll face. When you scale back, you decrease the intensity of your training sessions. Focus on flexibility, mobility, and easier runs so that you maintain fitness without stressing your body too much.

Figure 15.1 Race-Day Checklist

Got it?	Items needed
	Bag: tote, duffel, or backpack
	Race clothes and shoes
	Toiletries such as deodorant, cotton swabs, Vaseline, lip balm
	Cash (for parking, food on site, and so on)
	Photo ID
	Bib number (many races ask that you look this up on their website before you arrive)
	Change of clothes (including underwear)
	Change of footwear
	Towels (at least two to remove all the mud and dirt after the race)
	In-race fuel or food (bars, gels, blocks if your race will take you longer than one hour to complete)
	Plastic bags (as a laundry bag for dirty clothes)
	Postrace fuel (shake mix and bottle, bars, bananas in case you don't like the food options on site)
	Sunscreen (put some on before the race and reapply as needed, although avoid applying it near your eyes if you want to keep it from running into your eyes)
	Bug spray
	First-aid kit (yes, race organizers have these as well as medical staff on site, but it won't hurt to cover your bases and at least keep one in your car or bag)
	Bottled water

Pay special attention to any muscles that are sore or tight and may need some mobility and flexibility work this week.

Scaling back is known as tapering for a race. Some tapers start up to 2 weeks before a race, but for your purposes, a week should suffice. When tapering, do not rest too much. Continuing your regular training routine but decreasing your volume by 30 to 40 percent is generally advis ed.

If it isn't your first race and you have a series of races planned in a few months' time, you may not need to completely scale back the week before your race. Tapering and recovering after the race can get in the way of improving your fitness. Depending on the intensity of the race, some athletes continue to train all the way until race day. In some cases, a shorter race may provide more of a tune-up or opportunity to enhance obstacle-specific skills in preparation for a longer challenge. If it's your first race, this doesn't apply to you, but if you have several races planned over the season, adjust accordingly after you learn how your body recovers.

Two to Three Days Before the Race

Once your race is a few days away, you'll want to pay special attention to your diet. Try not to introduce any new foods at this point; keep your food intake comparable to what it has been throughout your training. The last thing you want is an upset stomach the day of the race.

Cut back on alcohol. Try to lay off all alcoholic beverages at least 48 hours leading up to your race. Consuming alcohol close to race day can dehydrate you more quickly than usual and can interfere with your quality of sleep. And you'll want to be rested and fresh for race day. So if you have any social events on your calendar, be sure to plan them in time to let the booze get out of your system several days before the race.

Two days before your race may be your final training day before the event. As much as you may want to cram in any last-minute strength, power, or endurance development for your race, don't. Take this time to focus on active recovery and ensure your body is mobile, rested, and ready for the challenge.

One Day Before the Race

With only a day to go, you should be excited! It's a good time to mentally prepare yourself for the race and listen to how your body feels after months of hard training. You don't have to work out today, but if you do, focus on flexibility, mobility, and other active recovery work. If you'd like to run the day before your race, limit it to no more than 30 minutes of easy running.

The night before your race, get plenty of good-quality sleep. You'll need to be rested up for race day. The exact amount varies among athletes. In general, get as much sleep as you normally need in order to be rested for an important day.

Race Day

It's the day of your race! All that you've been preparing for is finally here. Give yourself enough time to get ready and get to the venue. This includes allowing time to prepare and consume your prerace meal, gather any last-minute items, commute, and park your car. Wake up a minimum of 2 hours before the race to allow your body time to wake up, eat, digest, acclimate, and to get to your race with time to check in and warm up without stressing out.

For a prerace meal, go with the rule we introduced a few days before your race: Don't eat anything unusual or new that your body is not accustomed to. For some people, a healthy prerace meal may be toast and peanut butter with some fruit. Some may prefer a nutritious homemade shake. It's really up to you. Just be sure it's something filling enough to keep your stomach from complaining over the race but not so heavy that it will leave you feeling sluggish or nauseous. If you get a little hungry before your race, you can dip into the prerace fuel you've brought with you. When planning your prerace meal, give yourself enough time for food to digest before the race, usually a couple hours.

As most race organizers advise, try to get to the race at least an hour before your wave time. Give yourself time to park, check in bags, and make any last-minute prep details like a prerace snack (if the venue is far), a change of footwear, and a 10-15 minute warm-up before hitting the course. If it's your first race or a race you expect to challenge you, give yourself time to get your mind right and ready for the challenge—it's a lot harder to do that if you arrive at the venue with little time to spare before your start time.

Racing Etiquette

Millions of people now enjoy obstacle racing throughout the year, so you don't have the course all to yourself and need to be considerate of your fellow athletes. If you have experience with traditional road races, you may be familiar with the basic etiquette guidelines for racing, many of which apply to obstacle racing. Simply put, proper OCR etiquette can be summed up in five key rules.

❭ **Pay Attention.** Obstacle racing engages all the senses, so it's critical to be fully in tune with your surroundings. Leave your personal audio player at home. You'll need to be aware of the weather, environment, constructed and natural obstacles, and fellow racers. Be on the lookout for disguised obstacles like stickier mud, uneven running surfaces, and stray branches. Sometimes you can avoid the most common injuries simply by exercising caution and paying attention to the course. Barbed wire can be particularly hard to see when you're tired, so be cautious not to run straight into it.

❭ **Pace Yourself.** Pacing yourself not only relates to your speed or time on the course. You can use a good sport watch to ensure you are keeping a manageable running pace, but you'll also need your judgment to ensure a pleasant and successful race day. If you are a first-timer, don't sign up for a competitive wave. (If competitive racing is your goal, give yourself time to work up to it, familiarize yourself with the challenges of obstacle racing, complete several races, and build up your fitness and confidence before leveling up to competitive waves.) Be aware of where you are at the start line. If you are a fast runner, it's okay to be close to the front; but if you are new to the sport, start at the back so you can take your time and not worry about faster athletes having to step around you. This is where your sound judgment comes into play: If there is an obstacle you can't do, it's okay to skip it. But if you skip, keep in mind the next rule . . .

\ **Be Honest.** Often race organizers have a penalty in store for those who skip or cannot complete obstacles. Sometimes a volunteer is there to enforce it, sometimes not. If they're not, hold yourself accountable and do it. You signed up for the race and all that comes with it. Embrace your journey in its entirety. The penalties are there to help you improve your fitness and think twice about skipping an obstacle if it's out of some fear or slight reservation. Being honest also applies to competing in the wave you signed up for. If you get to the race really early, you may be tempted to sneak into the current wave, which may not be the one you registered for. Try not to. If it's a busy race, it may worsen bottlenecking at obstacles and diminish the experience for everyone.

\ **Follow the Golden Rule.** Be mindful of others. Think of how you would want to be treated if you were enjoying an obstacle challenge with other racers of various fitness levels. If someone is trying to pass you, step aside. Don't let your pride slow down your fellow racers. Also, step aside on the course if you need to do anything—tie your shoes, blow your nose, adjust layers. No scoffing at the less fit who are struggling with an obstacle. Remember the team-oriented roots of obstacle challenges and offer help when needed. Finally, if you see someone unattended or without a team who is hurt, help them get on-site medical attention.

\ **Enjoy the Race.** This should be simple enough, right? Maybe, maybe not. On race day, you may encounter challenges you just didn't anticipate. Don't let it ruin your enjoyment of the event, because the unexpected is what makes this sport so amazing. Give it your best, be confident in your training, and enjoy sharing the experience with your fellow obstacle racers.

Final Thoughts

As you can see, preparing for an obstacle race goes beyond your actual training sessions. Once you're a couple weeks away from your event, work on gathering all the items you'll need for the race. Prioritize those that you may need to shop for or order online. In the days leading up to your race, pay special attention to your diet to fuel yourself with the energy and nutritional needs essential for race day. Lastly, on race day, keep in mind our etiquette tips to maximize your own safety as well as those of fellow athletes. Following our item checklist guidelines, fueling suggestions, and etiquette tips will not only help prepare you for race day, but also equip you to enjoy postrace celebratory activities!

About the Authors

David Magida is the founder and general manager of Elevate Interval Fitness. Elevate provides group classes focusing on high-intensity interval training. In addition to its standard programming, Elevate also offers obstacle racing classes. Magida is certified through the American Council on Exercise and is a Spartan group exercise instructor. He is a member of the Spartan Race Pro Team and the host of "Spartan Race" on NBC Sports.

Magida has been racing OCR since 2011. In only his second race he found the podium for the first time and realized he had found his calling. It was only the legendary Hobie Call, a future world champion, who was able to outrace him over that course. That day Magida realigned his focus from training for triathlon races to singularly focusing on OCR.

Over the next three years Magida finished ranked in the top 10 in the Spartan Race Points Series (9th in 2012, 5th in 2013, and 10th in 2014) as well as other race ranking systems. He was one of the first 10 men in the nation to receive professional status. With 25 podium finishes in OCR events in total, including more than a dozen victories, Magida has consistently proven himself to be a threat to win every time he toes the line.

Magida has also demonstrated commitment to expanding the sport of obstacle racing with his involvement as a consultant for United States Obstacle Course Racing, a group which strives for unification of the major racing companies for the advancement of the sport. Magida is also a guest blogger for the Spartan Race Blog and Obstacle Racing Media.

Melissa Rodriguez is a fitness trainer, industry analyst, and obstacle racing enthusiast. She has held a personal training certification through the National Academy of Sports Medicine since 2003 and a certified strength and conditioning specialist designation from the National Strength and Conditioning Association since 2005. Although she trains clients with a range of fitness levels and athletic goals, she has a passion for coaching beginners. Rodriguez holds undergraduate degrees in English and biology as well as a Master's in Business Administration.

Since 2008, Rodriguez has served as a research analyst, report writer, and project manager for the International Health, Racquet & Sportsclub Association (IHRSA). As IHRSA's senior manager of research, she regularly presents research findings and opportunities at national and international conferences, and is a regular contributor to IHRSA's *Club Business International* magazine.

In recognition of obstacle course racing's potential, Rodriguez started following the sport in early 2011 when she trained and prepared a client for the Tough Mudder. Since then, she has maintained a blog on her website, MyExerciseCoach.net, which offers fitness and training guidance focused on obstacle course racing for beginners. Rodriguez is the author of the book *12 Weeks. 22 Workouts. Your First Obstacle Race*, and publisher of *Obstacle Race World: The State of the Mud Run Business*, the first-ever industry report on obstacle racing.